THE
CHEAT SHEET
OF
ITALIAN
STYLE

CONFIDENCE AND
SUSTAINABLE CHIC
IN TEN STRUTS

FRANCESCA BELLUOMINI

First Published in Canada Nov, 2016 by Italian Style Press
ISBN: 9780692810644

Typeset: Greg Salisbury
Book Cover Design: Jessica Gabrielle Lopez
Illustrator: Jessica Gabrielle Lopez
Portrait Photographer: Norma Gallegos

TESTIMONIALS

"What a wonderful, refreshing, and so... fashion book. Being in fashion a lifetime this is just a great book that brings so many memories and is a hit from the start to the finish. I so recommend this book and if you have traveled to Italy, you will feel now why you looked at the way they dressed and with such grace and ease. I hope my international alumni and fashion friends enjoy this walk through fashion."
Charlene Parsons - Director of Fashion Department – Miami International University of Art & Design

"Eight years ago, Francesca caught my eye in a room filled with women in Miami Beach. Although I couldn't put my finger on it at the time, when we met again later, and became friends, I realized that her inherent and natural sense of style was what set her apart in this city. Since we all want to be Francesca when we grow, this book came out just in time."
Barbara de Vries - Designer, environmental activist and author of 'Stupid Model'

"'The Cheat Sheet of Italian Style' debunks the myth of fashion as frivolous with wit and ironic prose. Belluomini describes chapter after chapter how style comes first and with it empowerment, confidence and a bit of attitude."
Aleksandra Lacka - Business strategist for entrepreneurs, founder of insights-studio.com

"A 'free-falling experience' indeed, 'The Cheat Sheet of Italian Style' is an unpretentious exploration of worldly flair that you can easily dive into. Francesca's transcending personality transforms into a book that is inviting, carefree, and most important uncomplicated. It's a no-hassle lifestyle companion that empowers us to pursuit our passions effortlessly with style."
Grace M. Castro - Founder of nonprofit organization Fashion Inspires More and Miami Fashion Film Festival

"In a world where trends and fast fashion dominate at the high cost of child labor and pollution, Belluomini talks to the reader with insight, wit, and a roadmap for a more sustainable fashion future. The CS of Italian Style is for any woman who said at least once in her lifetime "I have nothing to wear". Through personal anecdotes and her signature generosity of spirit, Belluomini makes the desirable Italian style accessible to everyone. A reader might not learn how to 'talk with her hands' but she will have all the ingredients to adopt the breezy, effortless attitude we see along the streets of Italy."

Gabriella Contestabile - author of 'The Artisan's Star' and 'Sass, Smarts, and Stilettos. How Italian Women make the Ordinary Extraordinary'

ACKNOWLEDGEMENTS

Thank you

It's Jim Rohn who once said: "You're the average of the five people you spend most of your time with." I am of the belief that your success depends on the people who believe in you, and here's is a heartfelt thanks to all who have supported my crazy idea of publishing a book, juggled with my frustrations, shoveled my doubts like after a snowstorm and held my hand to make my dream come true. I am thankful for all, including the naysayers and self-absorbed, who chose to dismiss my adventure, because, after all, they gave me the strength to succeed.

My daughter Cecilia, to whom I dedicate the book, goes first, as she defeats any orderly order for owning my heart.

My family: la mamma Brunella and il papa' Alfredo, my brothers Alessandro (with his wife Anna and their daughter Claudia) and Paolo, la nonna Titti. Il nonno Bruno and great grandmother Ebe because, even if they are no longer with us, they still live within me.

In alphabetical order: Laura Basso, Julian Chang, Melanie Cohen, Gabriella Contestabile, Cari Crucet, Angie Domecq Ferrer, Ed Estlow, Lara Galli, Elena Garcia, Lisa Halpern, Lourdes de Huilliard, Nicholas Charles Patrick Huxley, Marimar Molinary, Isabella Morselletto, Barbara G. Otero, Fernanda Pinzon, Luisa Rasia, Alex Raspberry, Steve Roller, Fabiana Vidlak Ildiz.

To all contributors, my legends and icons, for dedicating their wisdom, knowledge and time to make this book a gem. In alphabetical order: Alice Agnelli, Marianna Cimini, Vivia Ferragamo, Carlos Huber, Barbara Hulanicki, Orietta Marangoni, Stefania Marcon, Sabine Masi, Pietro e Federica Mazzettini, Rebecca Moses, Adriana Mulassano, Sally Perrin, Danny Santiago, Marta Vit.

The Cheat Sheet of Italian Style

A special bow to my publisher Julie Salisbury for believing in me and seeing beyond the book I told her I wanted to write, my talented illustrator Jessica Gabrielle Lopez, my insightful photographer Norma Gallegos, Fernanda Pinzon and Greg Salisbury who patiently dealt with picky me.

CONTENTS

FOREWORD

There are always truths in this world that we recognize subconsciously but don't reflect upon in our daily lives. The innate and inherent fashion sense of Italians is, for me, one of them. It is a national sensibility, upheld by all and is the pride of their global community.

And yet, until I had the honor of being asked to write this forward, I had never paused to think about it. How and why are Italians so inherently stylish? A simple week's vacation in Italy, surrounded by the architecture, the art, the food and the fashion, is enough to inform even the most casual of observers that the Italians do EVERYTHING with style.

I am more than a casual observer and in my 20 plus years as a fashion director, buyer, and consultant and sometimes designer, I have the great fortune to travel for work to the fashion capitals of the world. While each has their own particular specialties and qualities, there is nowhere like Italy, where an entire nation seems to have personal style bred into their very bones. Without reference to wealth, age, gender or occupation, it is as if every Italian wakes up and says "How can I personally make the world a more beautiful place today?"

How do they do it? And more importantly how can the rest of us do it? And by the rest of us I mean those of us born outside the Italian borders, without the Italian passport and the cultural DNA that appears to make all of it possible? Well, thankfully we now have this book to help us do it. Thankfully the rest of us non-Italians have Francesca!

I first met Francesca at the beginning for both of us. I was fairly freshly out of University with a Masters in Art History and not much experience in luxury fashion. Francesca was newly arrived in Miami and starting her sales career at La Perla. It may even have been her first day! 20 years of friendship and professional collaboration stand testament to the fact that at that very first meeting we instantly recognized kindred spirits. Bonding over lace, Lycra, prints and cuts, as we fashion girls are prone to do, was the start of something beautiful. Thanks to the wonders of social media, including Francesca's rising star on Instagram and her website, our frequent geographical distance has not impeded our ability to trade opinions and be influenced by each other's thoughts, tastes and discoveries. For me it is impossible to walk through Milan, Florence or Rome, without "seeing" Francesca on every corner. That undefinable style that every Italian girl seems to possess, merely hinting to me of all the qualities that Francesca, the most stylish Italian I know, exemplifies.

If anything, 20 plus years in Miami have made Francesca more Italian. Impossible perhaps you might think. But true! That old saying "when in Rome" can be reversed in her case. It's as if being out of Rome, so to speak, has made Francesca even more Roman! The daily comparison of living in America appears to have created an extra consciousness of the things that make up her national identity as an Italian, with her style being the clearest expression of all of it. As a fashion "star" she follows the designers and the trends and fashion culture. As an Italian, she never falls into the trap of blindly following the herd. I have long and secretly been envious of Francesca's ability to take the oldest thing in her closet and make it not only seem new and cutting edge, but also seem her own.

In reflecting on the place of Italians like Francesca as the leading style gurus of our culture, it occurred to me that I have quite a few French fashion-friends who would protest vehemently at this designation. But as dashing and sartorially fabulous as the French are, we have to recognize the place held by a culture that started with the Ancient Roman civilization and still influences us today. For a start, just google "gladiator sandals" and you won't need me to tell you that the Romans are still having an impact. Marco Polo with his far-reaching travels brought back the influences of global culture. These influences were absorbed into the very heart of Italian society, as still today designers look to other cultures for inspiration. And so it went on until Mr. Valentino and Mr. Armani brought that legacy of style to the entire world.

So what have those few thousand years since Roman times given the Italians style-wise that the rest of us can only hope to emulate? Confidence is one thing! Another is the knowledge that gladiator sandals may come and go as trends, but true style is forever. It is this knowledge that is at the heart of Francesca's expertise.

That Francesca has generously agreed to give us all this book, so that we too may have the tips, the tricks and the rules that every Italian learns as they grow up, is our great fortune. Read on and enjoy! You are about to learn everything you need to know about style from the quintessential Italian. A master of personal style.

INTRODUCTION

It wasn't until I moved to the States that I realized how Italian I actually was.

Not because I eat pasta or move my hands when I talk; my being more Italian than I think, hides in that flair, part genes and part heritage, that makes me look imperfectly polished even when going to the supermarket. Since friends, colleagues and readers have been asking for years, I developed the idea that the effortlessness of Italian style is achievable if adequately cultivated.

What defines Italian style and its quintessential seal of being pulled-together with insouciant elegance? Does wearing head-to-toe Gucci or Versace make you an Italian? How much of *la Dolce Vita*, Sophia Loren and Marcello Mastroianni, or Federico Fellini is still relevant?

I was born in Viareggio in the region of Tuscany, famous for the Firenze of Lorenzo de' Medici, Marquis Emilio Pucci and Guccio Gucci. The prevailing memory of my youth is that of playing dress-up with gowns and man blazers hanging in the enchanting armoire of my grandmother, nonna Titti. I never collected figurines or Barbies, but buttons from a special chest of drawers she owned. I could be left countless hours playing mother-daughter tea parties with my dolls, which I dressed with the leftovers from the gowns that my great-grandmother Ebe, a skilled seamstress, would make for her clients. It was my rabbit hole to wonderland; my own personal petites-mains and mini couture wardrobe that formed the sartorial foundation of unpretentious taste, which today pervades my Italian way.

Studying abroad and traveling nomadically until establishing myself in Miami, I continued to find joy in mixing local market finds with vintage discoveries and those sartorial staples that accompanied me everywhere.

"I love your style", immediately followed by "of course, you are Italian." Plus or minus any version of this has been a recurrent compliment in my twenty years of life in Miami. I have never been good at acknowledging compliments, but I knew I wanted to do something about it, besides simply showing gratitude and pride. Two decades on American soil made me too American for my Italian peeps, but still too Italian for the Americans. As my good friend Carson put it one day: "you are so Italian you don't even know how much." I moved from the mecca of Fashion (with a capital F) to a place that had everything, but glamour and elegance; the river of inspiration had ended at a screeching drought. But as a play on the old adage goes "you can take the girl out of Fashion, but not the Fashion out of the girl". My lifelong passion for fashion didn't expire, and the rest of me grew a bit unapologetic and quick-witted. I was wearing what pleased me without caring about what others thought I should or not wear.

It became clear that what comes natural to me, a chic effortlessness, was more of a personal realization that I was running out of time to keep the best clothes for a day to come, so I better wear them today; this quickly became my mantra.

Getting people acquainted to Italian style became a work of dissecting the way I dress in the morning, how I structure my wardrobe, what message I want to convey with what I wear, and why I feel good when I look good. Those who know me, know that I firmly believe "a moment cannot be mass produced," and that the same outfit, worn on different days by the same person, never does look the same.

What makes my style still truly Italian although I have lived half of my life abroad? How can I make it achievable for everyone? Is there a way to curate, study, learn, and become an apprentice of someone else's style? Is it genetic, within you from birth, or can it be acquired and cultivated over time?

Enthralled, I started looking for signs of what would make me choose one thing over another, ignore or despise something, the *non so che* - the French *je ne sais quoi* - that imprints my style as being so different from anyone else's. My way was not only perceived as different and desirable, but also unachievable, expensive, over the top, unexpected, and overall, a few notches more dressed up than required; Irreconcilable with my own way of being and thinking, since I have never felt overdressed. I've also never been known to be a fast and furious shopper. After a bad day, I much rather listen to Puccini instead of suppressing my sorrow with mindless shopping. I don't like to splurge on designer clothes; I frugally curate instead.

One more facet became evident: I do not follow the rules. All those must-haves, don'ts, never wear red with pink, buy this or die, contour and highlight, dress code required, the gender-defined frame of corporate attire didn't really mean anything to me. I would face them half bored and half peeved, baffled to see them as instruments to manipulate my style, homogenize it and keep it under "Uniform Patrol".

I had to begin somewhere, and the "what I knew it wasn't" sounded encouraging, and that was key. In fact, I don't have precise instructions to give, and you will not find the perfect recipe here to look like Cindy Crawford. While everyone should be one's own style curator, I am going to give you a palette and a brush of freedom with a patina of elegance and rigor, so as to let Italian style percolate through the cracks of everyday life to become your own curator. I imagine this book as a class with no homework, tests or finals, and more of a free-falling experience.

Style is not aspirational; it is not finding an Instagram OOTD (Outfit of the Day). Aspiring is not a sin, it doesn't make you the black sheep, but trying to figuratively fit into a certain look and ideally into a group or social enclave by emulating someone else, does make you stand out for all the wrong reasons. Your own taste and sense of appropriateness, personal preferences, physical attributes, mood of the day, and current lifestyle come first, and you need to own them with intelligence, passion and determination. I haven't been as confident all my life, on the contrary, I grew up doubting and seeing everyone else better endowed than me; thinner, better dressed, more spontaneous - if only I knew then what I know now, and I could bring those twenty plus years back.

A woman has that extra ace up her sleeve that positions her at a vantage point; I call it 'style with substance'. Style requires a good dose of attitude, freedom, strength, personality and character, and it doesn't only refer to the clothes or accessories you wear, it encompasses the roles you play on a daily basis, the hats you wear as a mother, daughter, entrepreneur, leader, manager, partner, wife, artist. Elegance has nothing to do with being well-dressed, but more with possessing a constellation of attributes.

While writing this book, I have spent innumerable hours with my ideal you, the imaginary reader that represents all of you, her name is Lennox. We went through closets, magazines, concerts, vacations and several lasagnas together. I put her to the test and she acquired the same nonchalance at putting together an outfit, as my grandmother manifested when making ragu (that laborious Italian meat sauce) dressed in her signature look – a silk pussy-bow blouse and pencil skirt.

It's my wish that you, Lennox, get all the ingredients (secret ones included) and learn to balance the doses at your own taste, enjoy the process at your pace, and confidently choose pieces to wear and introduce yourself with, that represent the best of who you are. There is no right or wrong. Well, there are indeed things you don't do, but they'll come at the end, when they will somehow sound already familiar to you. It should become like the Golden Ratio, the number of perfect proportions that exists in nature; a divine, invisible and irrational calculation that has fascinated scientists, inventors, musicians, designers for thousands of years. The Italian way should thus, begin to percolate throughout your style like a freshly-brewed cup of coffee.

You will also have the chance to meet my friend Leopoldo, a true Sicilian gentleman and ultimate bachelor, because we all imagine Italian men like him, even Lennox. He's that rare friend you go to for a style intel briefing, the one that mercilessly asks you, "what were you thinking with that outfit?" with the same tone he would propose to his girlfriend (and when he does propose, we would all be heartbroken), and who has the guts to stop you on your way out the door even when you think you are killing it with your outfit. I recurred to him too, because although he's been a nomad moving from Sicily to Dubai, from Miami to a stint in Rome and currently residing in London, he's an Italian at heart, and so "What would Leopoldo say?", will be our measure of the intangible quality of chic.

ONE

THE FOUR KEYS TO THE ITALIAN WAY

Four key concepts belong to this book like the rings to Saturn, and before proceeding onto our adventure of the wild unruly West of 'the Italian way', it's recommended we get used to them.

In no particular order the words are: style, fashion, trends and luxury. Whether you have your own opinion on them, find them confusing, insignificant or intimidating, they are commonly used, misused, abused or given the wrong meaning.

As with any other section of this book, each one is independent and stand-alone; I wanted to discuss these terms beforehand because, as you may imagine, they will be mentioned all throughout, and I wanted you to have a place to come back to and hit 'refresh', if need be. Make this your A, B, C of all-things fashion, the warp and the weft to weave your own Willy Wonka world.

STYLE

The idea of this book was born because of style at its raw state.

Style surpasses any love for fashion, shopping, trends, "it's putting our signature on the things that we wear and the way that we live," writes style priestess Rebecca Moses in her book, *A Life of Style*.

What's in style that fashion doesn't have?

In *The Vignelli Canon* by Massimo Vignelli, worldwide renowned Italian expert of graphic design says: "Style is a byproduct of a person's being. It reflects a way of thinking; […] style (or intellectual elegance) is the projection of a person's intelligence. Style is the tangible aspect of intangible things."

Style stands with intelligence, like vulgarity with illiteracy. Simplicity and humility bring enjoyment of possessions and their tangible result is elegance. Style has nothing to do with how much money you wear in an outfit, it moves hand-in-hand with taste, personal taste; it's not a question of "who was born first, taste or style?", it's a process of self-discovery that at one point makes its way through your closet. Style is the intangible quality of chic.

Style is elegance, understated and discreet, that makes us be remembered long after we leave, not just noticed. We all go to work, take a plane, car-pool and go to the gym, and the least of what we want is to fall into the dreaded uniform trap. No homogeneous sweat pants, black suit or comfy sweater will make us be remembered, unless we add some spice - the 'flavor of the day', if you will.

Getting dressed the Italian way is a ritual; A process of elimination, selection, a series of studied choices that make you look effortless; discovery in which the only common denominator is you. It's the thrilling sensation of listening to your mood when waking up and walking in the closet, not to look for a robotic response, but for stimulation and inspiration. Style is a continuous conversation with your wardrobe, which transforms a daily routine into a treasure hunt for the outfit that will be your best friend for that day. Owning your style will get you comfortable with the 'aha moment' of feeling empowered and confident that what you are wearing speaks the best of you. Being in a relationship with your style doesn't affect how you use your intellect, it's indeed the contrary; being confident with your style, makes you intriguing and attractive.

Style encompasses all aspects of our daily life, not just clothing, design or decoration. Style penetrates the way we travel, the food we choose, the magazines we read, and it stimulates assertiveness. You'll find many references to food and the pleasures of eating, because it is a quintessential element of true Italian style.

Style surrounds us in every detail and it speaks of us, from the silhouette of the car we drive to how we align irregular slices of bread to accompany an olive-oil tasting, from the choice of a skirt's length to the way we carry a new haircut. They may all appear to be haphazardly happening, but they are all choices. We need to pause, look around, and appreciate the details that become invisible to the eye with the fast rhythms we must subject our lives to.

THE TAKE-AWAY

An interview with Rebecca Moses to enrich the conversation on style.

Rebecca is a creative visionary at heart, and a fashion dignitary whose impressive pedigree has her excelling at fashion illustration for Vogue Italia, Marie Claire Italia, Fratelli Rossetti, and culminates with her book, *A Life of Style*. We became best Insta-friends, and she was gracious enough to allow me to interview her, for which I am grateful and happy to confirm that she survived.

Your career as a creative director and as an artist is a constant example of style. Your book, A Life of Style, is an empowering example of how to cultivate a life that goes beyond appearance. Where would you suggest we begin the path to find our own style?

RM: "Embark on a style journey like I suggest in my book. It's a form of style therapy! Reflect on your life, go back to the earliest memories and write down your most memorable memories, positive and negative. Putting pen to paper will explain a lot why we love and dislike what we do."

Your paintings, the "Mesdames", as well as your illustrations for Marie Claire Italia and Vogue Italia are the personification of style, they own a great deal of chicness, joyful spirit and bit of attitude. Are they inspired by real women?

RM: "They are inspired by two very important influences: 1. My world travels and the elements, people and senses that I experienced or recall. 2. I grew up to old Hollywood films. That dream larger-than-life way affected me and my vision of life, and the manner we live life."

There are countless ways to communicate your style, you illustrate over a thousand in the book, and one can use many, it's not limited to the way you dress. Does it change over the years, does it evolve with life?

RM: "Yes, some things change and some are constant. But we do evolve and need to evolve. The quintessential elements are there, but they do move forward depending on our life journey and the needs and desires we experience."

There are people with innate sense of style, how about everybody else?

RM: "The non- innate just have to work harder, but they will get the results! It's all about being honest to oneself, and keeping a good sense of humor and experimentation!

Does being confident in your own skin also mean not fitting into a stereotype, and ignoring definitions?

RM: "Yes, it is about accepting our own unique characteristics and manners and making them our 'signatures'!"

Is style perfection or imperfection? Tangible or intangible?

RM: "Style is our voice. It's very tangible. For some, it is imperfection; For others it's perfection; For some it's outrageous; For others it's sleek and dark ...."

Can you say style is like learning to play the piano, and when you start being playful with it, you own it?
RM: "In a way, yes. It is about venturing out of what you think people think you to be , and having the courage to step out and be what feels good for you!"

THE TAKE-AWAY: ENCORE

Iris Apfel, nonagenarian force of nature and icon extraordinaire, has maintained her unique style with such a passion that at the tender age of 94 still inspires generations.

Miami was chosen for the premiere of *Iris*, the documentary dedicated to her life, and we were lucky enough to have Mrs. Apfel herself for a Q&A time after the showcase. Fresh as a rose in the late afternoon of a traveling day, she answered questions with wit and sharpness, and all I wanted to do was hug her (which I didn't do). Taken by surprise by her presence and unprepared to ask anything, I didn't want to miss the opportunity and all that came out was: "Do you have a muse, an icon of inspiration?" - "NO!" with an expression equivalent to two capital letters was all I got as immediate answer. She later elaborated with something similar to what she says in the documentary: "The greatest fashion faux pas is looking in the mirror and seeing somebody else." Scrutinizing and copying celebrities or bloggers in their sponsored outfits, results in you looking bad, in her opinion. Thinking that dressing like someone who has been dressed for the occasion by a squad of specialists will make you look as good, is a huge detractor of your own self-esteem.

It all comes down to knowing yourself and, without falling into transcendental conversations, unapologetically looking at you in the mirror with honesty. Like with everything in life, transparency and unpretentious taste are the winning chips.

FASHION

I take fashion seriously, as much as Diana Vreeland was dead serious when, right after WWII, stated that "the Bikini is the most important thing since the atom bomb." Fashion is a loaded word. Fashion is a dream, storytelling, a slow process, an emotion, inspiration, interpretation and performance, a transmitted and decoded heritage.

Fashion doesn't have to please everyone, let Coco Chanel be an example when at the beginning of her career she displeased the crowds believing in the irruption she was making in the status quo.

When I first started, fashion was ephemeral, the land of the supermodels, gods and goddesses that were making the stories and inspirations of the designers real. Runways were twice a year for Ready-to-Wear and for Couture; there was no front-row galore of reality-show celebrities or influencers populating nonsensically the prime real estate. Fashion was a well-oiled system of traditions, buyers, journalists, Hollywood stars and editors, all doing their jobs. There was no model/Instagram prodigy, designers weren't creative directors, and stylists were working with the fashion editors in magazines, not being the stars behind the design of a runway collection. That was the world I fell in love with; where collections had designers (not creative directors) who had a vision for the season to come; seasons that spoke and inspired by means of colors, fabrics, mood boards, and a well-written story.

Now it's different. It can be intimidating, gossipy, frivolous, expensive, intricate, fascinating and complex, but fashion at its sartorial status has always been my happy world; since the time I would dive in my grandmother's armoire and play dress-up with exquisite garbs that my great-grandmother had made for my mother and aunts.

"Fashion is whispering, loudness is the new code, I prefer whispering," said Alber Elbaz in a fashion talk at Parsons School of Fashion.

"Anyone who lives within their means suffers from a lack of imagination" – Oscar Wilde

Elbaz is the designer who brought the French house of Lanvin back to the limelight from the dusty attic, and after 15 years got sacked after a hostile take-over.

Fashion is a drive, a well-crafted engine of creativity, craftsmanship, skills, dedication, traditions and heritage that becomes relevant in the present when translated through innovation. Yes! Quality, luxury, elegance and style are paramount, but undoubtedly there are signs of frivolity in it. "Listen to people and create a need that people don't know they need," continues Elbaz, in fact, "Fashion is not intellectual," said Elbaz, "it's like roasted chicken; you don't need to think to eat it."

Fashion is creating a dream that becomes true with a beautiful fabric, a sewing machine, and the skilled hands of a seamstress. It may sound outdated, but that is still the true meaning of fashion we will be indulging in.

Which girl doesn't take a dress-up play-date seriously? One too many times I have been addressed with sneering snaps such as, "that is woman talk" or "you and your little rags, you didn't need a Master's degree to go sell dresses". I hadn't realized how demeaning they were until years later, I shrugged them off my shoulders and into the "Ignore File" they went. My confidence boosted like how you feel when you play that youth fair game where you hit a weight with a hammer and if it reaches the top, a loud flashy bell rings. Following fashion no longer means that we are marked with the 'frivolous' tag.

If that which makes you refrain from fashion is your consideration of it being something irrelevant or distant, know that, your thoughts about fashion define who you are through what you wear, and becomes, whether you admit it or not, the first means of communication with others because we are continuously on display.

Embracing fashion and all it encompasses and balancing style with a great dose of substance, will only ease the path to your professional success, whether it's in finance, politics, or balancing family life or your passion for knitting. Your style pervades every aspect of your life, that's where Italian style takes place; it percolates like water, through the cracks of fashion and clothing, family, food, slow time, travel, art, history, curiosity, sandy beaches, opera.

In a moment of brilliant inspiration, and confined to the rush of 140 characters of a Twitter chat, I once said: "Fashion is the message; Social Media facilitates the message."

Fashion sociology taught me that fashion consists of two opposite forces - social identification versus distinction. We are pulled with equal strength by two different streams: imitate others to acquire a sense of belonging, or distinguish ourselves from others by uniqueness and individuality.

Which one prevails, relies solely on us.

Fashion is a merry-go-round where innovation and imitation go alongside. When a novelty trickles down and is massively adopted, it moves from innovation to imitation; it loses its status of novelty for the trend-setters, and that is when a new idea is needed. In the '90s these were considered the fashion victims, now they are blogger 'it' girls.

When the desire for change is imposed or succumbs to peer pressure, and is not genuinely longed for, taste and style are overcome by status-seeking attitudes. That is not what we are trying to accomplish here. The trick is to be content with the way you look, to be happy with your image, and to evolve with your life while not forgetting to smile.

Think of other women that you admire and to whom you can relate. And aspiring to a lifestyle a' la Duchess of Cambridge will only bring disillusion, disappointment and loss of self-esteem, since it was she who married into royalty, not you. So no, that's not what I am talking about. We can, however, admire her for her impeccable, soft, regal style, but how can we ever replicate that London aristocracy and international diplomatic jet-setting? This is where honesty and simplicity win over aspiration and false illusion.

I have elaborated the subject with Adriana Mulassano because she is considered the 'Pope of Fashion'. She is an establishment of the Italian newspaper Corriere della Sera, press officer for the Giorgio Armani of the golden years, and now professor at Rome's IED di Roma. She is convinced that "Fashion is culture and everybody is fasting of it." Without reading and forming a solid knowledge of the past, there is no future. My best friend Lara, with whom I shared my first pad in Milan during my first stint as a fashion insider in the early '90s that forged the beginning of me as an industry professional, was the gracious manner in which I was introduced to this private, reserved, most exquisite unique treasure of knowledge that is Mrs. Mulassano. Indulge in her interview, read and re-read what she says, and imagine me with a grinning expression, because I enjoyed the experience as one of the highlights of my fashion career.

Can Italian style be summarised into a definition?
AM: "I'd say it was possible. There were years, or better decades, especially between 1978 until the switch to the new century, in which Italian fashion was strongly characterised thanks to a group of designers who each brought forward a movement within their peculiar style consisting of profitable creativity, superb quality and constant research that overall, was conferring strength,

visibility and authoritativeness to the 'Made in Italy' mark. I'm obviously talking about the golden age, whose first authors were: Armani, Versace, Ferrè, Valentino, Missoni, Krizia, Romeo Gigli, and Dolce & Gabbana all with their original styles, Prada, Gucci…the simple names make us shake, so much that they contributed to the launching of the Italian style worldwide! France, sovereign till then, was put on its knees by our supremacy. However, things have changed today. Globalization, crisis, change of types of markets (decline of western markets and rise of Russian, United Arab Emirates and China), have led the big names still present on the market to face some changes that significantly compromised the image of our fashion."

The book contains tips on how to adopt the Italian style, do you think it is possible to learn from it?
AM: "Definitely yes! Because it is not a unique, but composite style. Within it, any woman can easily find her strong and decisive identity, in line with her body and taste. Or better yet, the one who loves sobriety, will become an Armani addict; the one who is looking for plenty of glamour in her way of dressing, will love Versace and Dolce & Gabbana; those who are fond of stylish avant-garde, will have no trouble in finding their match in Prada; ladies of the international jet-set, will find their mentor in Valentino; those who love a modern style, will be inspired by Gucci; intellectual women, will appreciate Missoni; and those who want to seduce with elegance and a touch of exoticism, will definitely pick Romeo Gigli."

Fashion and trends are forces that push in two different directions, true or false? Which one should we follow?
AM: "My opinion is firm. If a woman wants to be truly elegant, she must never take one or the other as the Bible, but rather keep in mind both of them, drawing from them the traits that make her unique, individual, unrepeatable as flaunting a personal style. Exceptions can be (partial) given in to fashion colours, trendy accessories, but with parsimony. Each of us, provided we want to be elegant, must know very well how to create our style even without being the Venus de Milo! In this respect, I am worried, and a bit shocked, in seeing how young generations especially, but not only, adopt anything that's trendy without a minimum of self-irony, self-control, and therefore style. The result is that roads, offices and parties are crowded by oversized ladies and young girls squeezed in leggings without style, short women standing on 15-cm heels and wedges, young women with Latin legs showing them off in unacceptable short shorts and mini-skirts, sometimes with glitter! It's not hard to imagine the harm they do to themselves!"

Did democratization of luxury bring more style to the streets or, on the contrary, restrict it to catwalks?
AM: "First of all I state that there hasn't been a democratization of luxury. This concept implies that luxury producers are selling at prices affordable by everyone! This is far from the truth. Instead, an imposing phenomenon occurred, ascribable to the low cost of labour in Eastern European and Asian countries, which led luxury prototypes to be copied and compromised in style. Therefore, made accessible to a large public through low-cost distribution in millions of stores and markets worldwide. I wouldn't call it democratization, but rather bad diffusion. Because we can't ignore that the copy of a dress tailored with a low quality material and sewn even worse, causes a relevant damage to luxury and style. If I think that up to 50 years ago, anyone who wanted to reproduce a High Couture model from Paris or Italy for its customers, had to buy the paper pattern at high cost from the same tailor; I can't say that a step forward was made in diffusing good taste!"

Is there any woman that you consider a worthy representative of the essence of the Italian woman?
AM: "This is no longer the age of icons like Marella Agnelli! Certainly in Italy there are many elegant women, much more compared to other countries. But none of them sets trends or is recognized as prototype of Italian essence. This is the positive aspect of democratization! A paradox, but it is."

With many years as an expat, I reached the conclusion that Italian style is a harmonious mix of culture, art, design, imagination, creativity and passion. Your career and books, Mrs. Mulassano, are evidence that culture takes the first place. When do other elements come into play?
AM: "It's all true, culture lies at the origin of any job well done. How could I have written about fashion with authoritativeness if, before starting my job as a critic, I had not read tons of books on the history of past and current fashion? Knowledge of the subject is a requirement. But this condition isn't enough; Sector culture is essential, as well as culture concerning art, custom and design, all which allow you to constantly relate one discipline to another, make appropriate quotes, credible and pertinent comparisons. But even all of the above is not enough. Fashion must exercise a flair on you, otherwise you don't understand it and can't express opinions. In conclusion, I admit it, I've always been fond of fashion, a love that gave me the push to approach it first, and then make it part of my life since I was 20 years old!"

TRENDS

Trends are transient. Now we live in the generation of the selfie, where trends are born and die as fast as a lightning bolt through the Instagram feeds of 'it' bloggers (also known as influencers); the ones with hundreds of thousands of followers. According to universally known Laver's Law, a trend is 'daring' before it becomes 'smart', and dies when it becomes 'ridiculous'. Back in the late '30s, when this rule was defined, it was revolutionary and it was barely used for fashion. Twenty years ago, the shelf life of a fashion trend had a survival rate of a good 18 months, and not from the moment it came out on the catwalks, but from the moment it hit the stores until the new corresponding season would come out. Twenty years after, technology and global communication shortened the process to a calculated and paid-for series of blog posts, several social media images, some of which are called 'selfies', creating a phenomenon called the *democratization of luxury*.

The idea is self-explanatory and terrifying, as it brings along the controversial issue of fast fashion as opposed to slow fashion. Practices of sustainability, fair trade, quality, craftsmanship, tradition, conscious buying and hand-made, ensue.

Fast fashion, is the activity where retail chains capture the most sellable new creations that go down the runways during what's known as, Fashion Month (New York, London, Milan, Paris and repeat), immediately copy them and make them available as a knock-off at a fraction of the cost of its original designer's price. Fast fashion breaks more rules that one can think of, creating a ripple effect that has 'bad' written all over. Low-cost production, intellectual property infringements, exploitation of labor (even below-the-age labor), unhealthy conditions, pollution, rising levels of carbon footprint (fast fashion is the second most polluting industry in the world, according to the U.N.), all to make available to the masses what otherwise wouldn't reach them. Hence, the controversial concept of democratization of luxury.

What would Leopoldo say?
He was on his scooter heading to the South Kensington indoor pool when he told me:
L - "Why uselessly spend all that money on a pile of rubbish that won't even survive long enough to bring it to the dry cleaner's once?"
Enough said.
Slow fashion is a movement that encourages the use of time to embrace the design process. It

separates the creative phase of inspiration, design and research, from that of production and consumption. More than a business model, it's a movement; it's reinvigorating enough to embrace it as a lifestyle - from 'slow fashion' to 'slow food', the step is quite close.

In my preteen years, I think I was 11 or 12, my father told me something that stroke a chord and grew with me, he said: "We don't follow trends, we set them". A rather snobbish saying that this Italian girl goes by today; One that strives to be as appropriate as possible with a pinch of attitude, savoir faire.

Is the current status a period where trends are dead? Why should we want to be told what to wear when we know what we want?

'Trendy' is an utterly annoying word, as screechy as a black chalkboard. It brings to mind that time when at 17 I was prompted by pure peer pressure (read: my first boyfriend) to fit in a popular high school group called, *i Paninari*. Becoming one, implied knowing someone who would ease me into 'the gang', and an initial financial commitment that exceeded my allotted budget for my Levi's 501 and Timberlands - which as worker gear imported from the U.S. weren't cheap - , a Moncler puffer, and a multicolor striped Shetland crew-neck sold at a posh exclusive boutique in downtown Firenze. I stopped at the Levi's 501 and got bored. Then the boyfriend, moved by generosity, did the boyfriend thing and eventually bought me the sweater and the shoes. I would only wear them when I would hang out with the crew. I still own them and cherish them as a reminder of the time when my sense of personal style was filed under 'fail, learn, and never repeat'.

THE TAKE-AWAY

As you may have gathered, we don't vouch for trends in here. It's not rebellion, we just ignore them. If you practice the exercise of ignoring the trends, fashion automatically becomes less intimidating, expensive and imperative, and more like a canvas - an impressionist's garden.

LUXURY

"Luxury is a necessity that begins
where necessity ends" - Coco Chanel

Luxury has become the norm to aspire to.

Masstige, is the new noun conceived to express the junction of mass production with prestige; where luxury products are diluted and made available to the broader consumer market. *Masstige* products lurk in where disposable income allows the acquisition of aspirational goods; a world where a pair of sunglasses, a wallet or a purse, buys one step into a higher status.

Owning exclusive-looking products has become affordable, thanks to fast-fashion brands that do a great job at replicating designer garments; mostly infringing intellectual property rights, sustainability principles, ignoring quality, craftsmanship, dedication and fair-trade, to perpetrate consumerism at its crude state. This is the point where luxury is no longer luxury.

Twenty years ago, Giorgio Armani brought his understated style and androgynous elegance to America's middle-market via Hollywood, and pioneered the current celebrity-driven system by hiring socialites of the likes of Lee. It may seem strange now, but nobody had thought

"Elegance is refusal."
– Diana Vreeland

of it before; Infiltrate Hollywood's high society as a validating ticket to then trickle down to the ideal customer and lure them into shopping. That year he approached the stars before the Oscars red carpets, and the system was disrupted forever; one way ticket, no return.

Today, twenty years later, we live in the era where luxury can be constructed and faked, thanks to publicists, managers, celebrity stylists, representation contracts, social media, fashion immediacy, exclusivity and model stardom. Everybody owns a piece of luxury, whether it is in the form of a perfume, a wallet or a purse.

Italian style doesn't discriminate those who wear luxury from those who don't, at least those who cannot afford it, because the Italian way is, contrary to popular belief, extremely discreet and understated. 'Made in Italy', is based on the principles of premium quality, craftsmanship, heritage and research, attention to details, tradition and innovation, and they are all lined up in small quantities, like homeopathic pills.

Luxury becomes a state of mind; It means owning your personal style, never regret wearing something, feeling appropriate and at ease, regardless.

One day, my daughter asked me the Italian words for 'cheap' and 'expensive'. When I told her there's no word for 'cheap' in the Italian vocabulary, she busted into a loud laugh: "Of course, you guys don't do cheap". I can't deny my mama-duck-raffled-feathered-chest feeling of having created a perfect mini me who, at age 16 and being brought up in the Magic City where everything is plastic, money, surgeons and shoes, appreciates a quality product, whether we can afford it or not.

My grandfather used to say: "who spends more, spends less." The real luxury is recognizing quality over quantity, it's first a state of mind.

THE TAKE-AWAY

We are not here to judge people based on how much money they wear. Luxury is not showing the money you have by what you wear, it's seduction that surpasses the product you wear or food you eat. You know that saying: "You are not rich, until you can fly on a private jet without posting a picture", in other words, you do what you want and you keep it for yourself. The indulgence lies in the enjoyment, not in how many thousands of people you show it to.

Italian style and food go hand-in-hand because there's no separation, we like the good things and we take them seriously. Same way there's no closet without a blazer, there's no kitchen without olive oil. The Mediterranean Diet became a thing along the years, and people started appreciating all the things that were my native food staples like red wine, Parmesan cheese and olive oil.

To confirm this path where food and fashion run parallel through the track of luxury, I interviewed Gabriele Corto Moltedo; Born in a family of traditions, he took the commitment to craftsmanship and design to the next level by founding his eponymous handbag and accessories brand. Influenced by the world of music and inspired by New York, where he was born and studied, he now lives between Paris, Venice and Florence while also overseeing the family's new endeavor; An estate in Lake Bolsena, Italy, that is a jewel boutique farm that produces a special olive oil called, RES ANTIQVA (Latin for the old way).

Let's play a game and live an imaginary life of two parallel worlds, olive oil and clothes, slow food and slow fashion. An ideal life of luxury is made of quality meaningful actions that encompass all senses, which is choosing quality over quantity. Are there such things as Couture and High Street in the olive oil business?

GCM: "I think that there surely is a Couture and High Street, if you think of the fashion example: one in couture would basically know the pattern maker and the seamstress that took the time and patience to make that one off-piece, while on the other hand, the fast-moving lower-price fast fashion relies on the mobile supply chain that follows the cheapest labor and favorable currency to deliver a product that has the resemblance of that of a normal garment, with little to no accountability for the provenance and conditions to make it. We have the same in the olive oil business, there are small farms all over the Mediterranean that produce quite good product with little to no economy of scale, and then there are the giant food-chains that misrepresent the product they are selling at a very low mass-price, whilst mislabeling it and not being clear on provenance or composition; Getting by, taking advantage of loopholes in system of checks.

How did you become an olive oil maker?

GCM – "I'm a huge foodie, so when my family acquired an estate on Lake Bolsena, we decided to try crushing the olives on the centenary trees found on the grounds. The taste was enchanting; we fell in love and decided to carry on the tradition that had already begun centuries ago, to make pure extra virgin olive oil, the old way- the Res Antiqva way.

Making olive oil is knowledge, manual labor, traditions, skills transmitted through generations, and technology that needs to keep up with newness, how do old and new reconcile?

GCM – "Very simply, I think we are in a better position today as far as making olive oil, than we were, let's say, 100 or even 40 years back. The core today still lies in manual labor, but machine aided. Where before to get the olives off the trees farmers would beat the trees with sticks, now we caress them with soft silicone tubes that gently rub the olives of the tree and gently drop them into the same nets that have been used for generations. The pressing is more complex and probably much more efficient, as we are able to capture the essence and maintain it for a longer time through advanced and controlled storage techniques that don't alter nor disturb the oil.

(I must interrupt here for a moment of reflection: when we were kids we used to help the farmers beat the trees, it was harder than a boot camp, rest assured. Don't you tell me this is not poetry, a hard, strenuous physical job the way he described it, looks as gracious as ballet, he's like 'the olive oil whisperer'.)

If craftsmanship lies as a foundation of the perfect blazer, what makes the perfect batch of olive oil?

GCM – "A few indicators that make for a good oil are: 1. The variety of the olive trees used, the composition of the blend, for example at Res Antiqva we use the Caninese variety mixed with Frantoio and Leccino to create our blend. 2. The time that it takes to crush the olives from the moment they drop to the ground; At Res Antiqva we allow a maximum of three hours to go by from tree to press, like a fresh juice, we seal the antioxidant properties into the bottle. 3. Knowing when to pick the olives from the tree, not too soon, not too late. Just at the right moment. If you pick them too early, they will be too harsh and give off that spicy, almost tongue-burning, effect. If you pick them too late, you will dilute the flavor of the oil as the olive will have matured too much just like a fruit, and no one wants the rotten pear. Do they? It has to be just right - beautiful, fragrant, fresh."

Can an exquisitely tailored suit or bag make life taste better like a good slice of country bread with extra virgin olive oil?

GCM – "I think both can bring joy to the beholder, yes of course."

An Italian home is not complete without a bottle of olive oil, as well as a closet is not complete without ...?
GCM – "Your grandma's white crochet linens."

Is there olive oil etiquette; something that you never do?
GCM – "1. Never waste! 2. I would say you never burn garlic in the oil or you ruin your pasta and your oil. 3. If it's good, don't use it sparingly!"

TWO

DON'T TAKE YOURSELF TOO SERIOUSLY

Getting dressed is fun, not a chore; fashion is a direct language.

They say "life is too important to be taken seriously," a true paradox, and when it comes to the Italian way of getting dressed, a great dose of humor, irony and madness comes as dead serious as your morning cappuccino.

The way it all translates into style can be summarized in one straight instruction: don't end up in the Reddit file on male advice called, *Fashion Pictures that Make you Want to Punch People in the Face*. Reddit is a free entertainment website where content is populated by its own community members, resulting in sometimes outrageous requests and absurd threads that can be active for years. To give you a figurative example of what fashion is not, feel free to access the file and scroll through the pictures. Be advised that it's an open-access site; the content is unfiltered, so mean-spirited comments are to be expected. What I am trying to convey is that when moved by the fortitude of your inner style and confidence in your own skin, you will never come across as ridiculous, inadequate or worse, costumed. The secret lies in not looking stupid while you do it all with nonchalance.

Do you know your style?

'Chic' is not a look. This word has been relegated to a corner where flashy logos meet street style. There is no premeditation in chic. Chic just happens. It's intangible. You can perceive it, much like the way wisteria blossoms or the way a jacket is casually thrown on a chair; from the fluently elegant manner a shawl is wrapped around the shoulders to the way you effortlessly serve a humble meatloaf.

This might be the most appropriate moment to share a snippet of a conversation I had with my friend Vivia Ferragamo over WhatsApp (because BFFs do that, we don't only check out each other's shoes).

Is 'chic' something universal, or what's chic for me may not be for someone else?

VF – "Can we define 'chic'? Is it having a certain knack for dressing a la mode, having an attitude/style? I think one is born chic; it's how you carry your body, how you listen to what feels good, it's an outside reflection of the inside you. It is confidence and feeling good in one's skin!"

You are saying it's more of an allure, somehow intangible, right? You don't buy 'chic', but to be chic you don't do cheap …

VF – "Nothing to do with cheap … chicness comes from within! It's in one's DNA!!!"

So far, we've learned style has nothing to do with fashion, chicness comes from within and now, take this, don't take yourself too seriously - a tried and true recipe filled with traps and delicate maneuvers that take you closer to the Italian way.

A reality check: make peace with the fact that what you were wearing in your early twenties is not what you should still be wearing in your forties, with one exception: your Levi's. God bless you if they still fit. It has nothing to do with labeling, discriminating, ageing, but as life progresses, style evolves, adapts, rises (hopefully) to higher standards, and advances in sophistication and confidence. Meanwhile,

"I want my ashes scattered at Bergdorf's"
– Victoria Roberts

the law of gravity plays its role in working its way down with your skin, and that's when you start understanding that the best thing you should do with those eye wrinkles and saggy knees is gracefully accept them, instead of fighting them back with some insane plastic surgery.

How do you dress the Italian way?

Wear what makes you most at ease, with irony and sense of humor. Remember to always have fun.

There's nothing more annoying and a bigger turn-off than someone trying hard to belong to a clique, and as women we are well aware of who these people are. It's like being the popular girl, (Blair Waldorf from *Gossip Girl*), and being surrounded by wannabees, it all results in a gigantic waste of time and energy, yielding very poor outcomes.

Create a relationship with your own wardrobe. Remember it's not the clothing that dresses you, even when you must wear scrubs or a lab coat at work. I went through the painful process of wearing a uniform when I worked in retail for a leading luxury leather goods company. It was a sad combination of garments, chosen to be equally wearable for women or men, and immediately learned how the one-style-fits-all is just a big lie. It felt like being in a Marxist commune, or inside an all-grey colony of rapid moving ants. Corporate used it as a fishnet to entrap the employees in the idea that it was a privilege to wear garments made by *la maison*. However, this "privilege" restricted to be worn exclusively inside the premises of the store, dry cleaning services were scheduled to pick up and deliver several times a week, belongings were safely guarded in a locker that was still property of the company after we left. My work life became a grey and navy blur, albeit my favorite colors.

Those were the days when I didn't feel particularly good wearing whatever we were told to wear in order to endure the daily tasks of the boutique, and my performance followed suit - sales were slow, I wasn't confident, didn't look sophisticated enough for customers to trust me and buy a $20,000 bag off my recommendation. How could they? I looked like their driver, at best; we looked ridiculous in those ill-fitting uniforms.

I may come across as entitled or unappreciative, I mean after all, I was being asked to perform a job wearing clothing that were made in Italy and chosen by the same designer I was praising while selling merchandise. But my experience there was as robotic as filling egg chocolates in a factory. Clients wouldn't even recognize me when they'd meet me at events outside the boutique - at those events I was me, inside the store I was a uniform.

My story is not isolated. Through the course of my career as a style consultant, I have encountered and made friends with numerous women who have gone through a similar path to failure. It begins with the infamous Employee Handbook, written in human resources lingo that tries to lure you into "corporate attire" with the same emphasis that a farmer would send their youngest child to collect eggs for breakfast from the chicken coop. Except for safety hazard gear, the rest of what you are allowed and obliged to wear is equivalent to conformity. Results can be as disastrous as dress-code anxiety, a limited uninspiring repertoire, and the constricting need to hide the sensual, creative, communicative side of any woman's brain and soul.

Some public sectors and most conservative corporations allow you to wear nothing but black, which creates an unfortunate chain reaction. Having to buy clothing is wrong, a contradiction in terms, because getting dressed is part of one's language, personality, education, inherited habits that all pitch in the final result, which equals to one's style. Shopping can turn from being a pleasant, freeing experience, into a painful workout routine (and you know the one thing that Italian girls have in common with their French counterparts? We don't exercise.)

The process of looking and trying on garments that don't correspond to one's idea of style and personal taste, tend to turn unappealing, like that vegetable soup that you had to gulp down for dinner because "otherwise no dessert". When eventually said clothing enters the wardrobe, they will most probably occupy a small obscure section of the closet and remind you of work, and how much you would like to look good to impress the boss if only you could do it on your own terms. At the bottom of the domino effect is work performance: the stress of being boxed in a business-like situation ends up influencing the very results we are expected to produce.

I find FIT's latest exhibition title, *Uniformity*, fit to the purpose. It explores uniforms as the antithesis of fashion; where one end pulls for stability and functionality, and the other pulls in the opposite direction of innovation and creativity. As much as uniforms are meant for the wearers to blend (like mine in my retail stint), they also make the wearer stand out (think of a navy cadet or an army general). Fashion draws inspiration from both of them, think of the poetry behind denim overall and a Jean Paul Gaultier blue blazer and gold buttons "borrowed" from the Marines.

Italy went through one of the most terrible and unforgiving moments in its history with Mussolini imposing uniforms in schools and in public sectors that were meant to impose discipline, but the Italy where I was born and raised never had any school uniforms; except those worn at private schools, reserved for the few rich kids.

When I was given my first-ever Employee Handbook, my I-don't-follow-the-rules mind went ballistic. Why must we not sign a contract because employment is "at will", but I must abide to something called 'corporate attire'? My head started spinning from all the unanswered questions. Here I was, born in Italy, where fashion as "ready to wear" was born and had never heard of such a definition, and what was I supposed to do to fill this hollow definition with sense? (Add a sneering face, because I am Italian and can't help it).

Immediately following that cold shower, came the realization that I had to forget my creativity and love for getting dressed in the morning; the designer pieces accumulated with years of sample sales, my vintage dresses, my heels and made-to-measure sandals, because nothing was conforming to any uniform standard. Denial was my first instinct. For the first month, I refused to penetrate the obscurity and antiquity of said 'corporate attire' until I was called to attention for wearing a big misunderstanding; I was verbally warned for wearing the simplest flat sandals made-to-measure by an international designer brand.

Panic ensued in the precise expression "I am going to get fired for wearing my clothing", followed by plain depression. The only remedy I found feasible was to reduce my workwear to the small right corner of the closet, the dark one,

"You can never be overdressed or overeducated"
– Oscar Wilde

21

and shrink it down to a mere ten pieces and two pairs of shoes. That same period I put on weight. I didn't like what I was seeing. I had no inspiration in the morning, everything was boring and insignificant, and all because of that definition drilled in my head that had blindly forced me to an unwanted direction. As with every problem there is a solution, I was able to come out of the cage by respecting the rules, revitalizing my sense of style, taste and personality, without being written-off ever again. Actually, this time around, my productivity and performance followed suit manifesting rewarding results. I wouldn't be here telling you "you can do it", if I hadn't personally gone through it first. Living in my fashion bubble wouldn't have allowed me to even realize the daily struggle that women experience with working in a male-dominated environment. The truth is, no matter how much I had scaled down my way of dressing from what apparently seemed flamboyant and not corporate-friendly, people would still compliment me; you know very well that when women compliment you it's either out of infinite jealousy, or it is the most profound truth. I have never been good at acknowledging praise and appreciation to the point of seeming impolite, but that was indeed the turning point. I couldn't deny my reputation for the "one that is always looking good" and my payback became … the seed of this book. While the right corner of the closet destined to workwear expanded, my confidence and sense of belonging strengthened procuring a Pinocchio domino effect, professionally, physically and psychologically from the wooden toy, I became a kid in flesh.

The same reasons apply if you decide to copy someone out of insecurity, jealousy or to acquire a misleading sense of belonging. Opting to copy someone because of an Instagram post or because you aspire to reach their lifestyle, is a costly chain of bad news. Your features and flaws are only yours, and what makes someone look good could be a poor choice for you. Take for example a pair of high-waisted jeans: they will look totally different on short muscular thighs, than on someone with long thin limbs. The same goes for a cropped top on a flat chest, or on a round belly. Where's the fun in copying someone? Nowhere. I say it again; dressing up should be fun, not a chore.

Get it from the Italians, mix a good dose of irony with happiness and common sense, and for the rest, there's nothing a good coffee cannot fix. When you buy a dress, choose your right size. There is no reason to go smaller to look sexier and show off your legs. First, the Italian way is more sensual than sexy. Second, the seamstress will do the alterations if needed. Third, why should you miss the chance to order that delicious linguine agli scampi just because your belly will pop out of that two-sizes-two-small bandage dress? And I haven't made this up. I have friends and acquaintances doing that while barely confessing it. You know my reaction by now - from incredulously astonished to pity, because there's no way in hell I would turn down pasta for the sake of a bandage dress. Do the opposite and I promise double joie de vivre.

Put a smile on it.

Über-stylist and Vogue Japan Fashion Director extraordinaire, Anna Dello Russo, made an ironic and flamboyant 'Fashion Shower' video in the occasion of a one-time collaboration with high-street chain H&M. While dancing, laughing and having the time of her life (and she is always the soul of the party), she recites ten commandments that turn out being a shower of fashion: wear a coat as a dress, do a little dance before getting dressed, accessorize like there is no future, to name a few.

Dello Russo is not your typical working girl, like you and I, she is the extreme example of the Italian girl that doesn't take herself too seriously, yet takes her wardrobe as seriously as we take tax day. She owns two apartments in Milan because her clothing collection cannot be secluded in storage like the rest of us commoners do, not to mention she is said to use the kitchen as an extra closet. Fashion is her alphabet, she doesn't think twice about changing in her car while the driver takes her from one show to the other during fashion week; no hesitancy with admitting she owns 4000 pairs of shoes; she takes her wardrobe dead serious, yet she has fun while getting dressed; no pant is too wide, no skirt is too short.

Don't forget to smile. A solar, open, brilliant and maybe even unmistakable laugh, solves even the most intricate situation, like a ripped sleeve or an undone hem.

What would Leopoldo say?
L: "You have to dress to please yourself first and you'll always feel at ease wherever you are. From saying it to doing it, there is a sea of nuances; you certainly need a great deal of confidence."

Know your style, keep the aplomb, be a flâneur, stay away from posing, photo-shopped images, emulating. Form follows function: a genteel way of dressing doesn't look affected. If you have a pinky ring with your family emblem, you wear it with blue-blooded aplomb and don't bling it out. Keep your sense of identity, and don't let peer pressure or social media antics influence you.

THREE

START FROM THE ESSENTIALS

After years of accumulating many clothes, cards, toys, games that reminded me of something so bad that I had to rent a storage unit to host them, I ended up learning a very valuable lesson. Those boxes, no matter how well sealed and catalogued, were guarding the cherished content like a fort; the maximum level of attention they got was when they were moved from one storage unit to another. Then they'd be lovingly placed in the new home, still unopened. After one too many moves and the inevitability of lost boxes, I came to realize that the memories, sweet and sour, romantic and maternal, were still vivid without looking at them, touching them, feeling them or smelling them.

The American version of me and my wardrobe, for years, fought a war made of battles of contradiction. My start was good when I first moved from Italy, with a clean slate of two suitcases holding la crème de la crème, my precious treasures, my winter and summer Italian lives. The relationship became complicated, alternating shopping binges and relapsing into mindless buying every time I would try to clean up. I lived in a continuous state of love-hate that I couldn't shrug off my shoulders; there was always another dress lurking and plenty of luring space for it. However, despite the army of clothes hanging, too many at the same time, washed and dried or amassed on the bench at the foot of the bed, I still had nothing to wear. Abundance was not only prevalent in the closet, but it also pervaded the kitchen, turning out to be a chaos of fast fashion and junk food. I no longer knew where my clothing was coming from, or whether the food I was ingesting had been chain-manufactured or grown locally.

It gets even more interesting.

I personally reached the point of no return when I got pregnant. While my body started altering its shape and morphing, I found myself forced to choose between the widest array of choices available for purchase in the maternity section, and my less-than-minimal interest in indulging in any of them. The sizes were exaggerated, the offer was overwhelming, fabrics and materials were irritating, horrible and gross. At least that's how I expressed my hormonal disgust to the poor sales lady who never found a more difficult expectant (Italian) prospect.

As the silkworm in the cocoon, through the nine months, I created my own ideal wardrobe;

the pregnant version of it. One where stretch knit long dresses, jersey skirts and T-shirts formed the foundations, and tunics the complements; shaken not stirred with the then-husband's sportier shirts, cardigans, and sweat pants.

Comfort, simplicity and taste were the inspiring catalysts to what turned out to be a proportionally-built small wardrobe. My maternity capsule collection was a lesson on so many levels and it had its perks; the birth of my daughter standing unparalleled above all. I was pregnant and my cathartic moment was facing the progressive growth of the protuberance, whatever moment in your life becomes pivotal for a change, that's where you should leverage. There is no more or less important or trivial moment of truth in life, your current self wants to feel good and dress to kill. There is no mid-measure or compromise, only a plain solid crisp-looking you.

The first major lesson was facing how silly and incongruent I was falling victim to the temptation of the junk wardrobe; the vicious circle of buying for the sake of following subconscious instincts prompted by mag ads or the tease of the year-round sale. A closetful of poor choices was a bad mistake that cost me double the money; what I needed for the time being, mixed with my old loyal staples, plus all I had to replace after coming back to my body and disposing of the old junk. With the judgement of the years gone by, I should have remained loyal to the Italian way, instead of letting the rookie enthusiasm of living in a place where everything was available at any given hour, prevail. However, had I been disciplined, I wouldn't have gone through that self-discovery path, or found the empowering light to realize how simple it is and how complicated I had made it.

The second was the realization that I had survived the period with grace, simple elegance, peace of mind, and a handful of garments forced into reverse gear back to my Italian truth - "who spends more, spends less". There is something fascinating about simplicity, the fullness with nothing more and nothing less.

There you have it, despite having the Holy Grail of wardrobe perfection ingrained in my blood, I had no immunity, and I got infected with the misleading shopping therapy bug, went to rehab, paid in frustration and financial strain, and came out with my chip clean again. It doesn't matter where you are in the process, you can do it, and by that, I don't mean to get pregnant. As the simple and natural occurrence of birthdays rolling out, any event in life that changes rhythms, status, location, job ranking or mental disposition, is the trigger of a liberating and empowering new phase of life.

I can't tell you how many times I went through cleansing sprees since the first one that happened after my pregnancy, because I lost count. I know that the thrill of 'new' is as energizing as a snake shedding its skin, not that I know how the snake feels, but I know that it means new life and potent energies of renovation through the pores.

Assess who you are, what your lifestyle is, what has changed, recognize your evolution, inner growth, role and aspirations. Face the process with the same seriousness and nonchalance you would use at the appointment with your hair colorist; remain open-minded and trusting. Before you even reach the moment of truth and the elimination starts, a realization must manifest itself like a light bulb over your head; you are in a place of pleasing or hiding yourself with clothing that represent just the minimal amount of 'good enough'. It's time to move on. This is the time when you discover who you are at your own pace. Just know that when you initiate the process, you are ready to come to terms with what does fit and no longer fits with your character. This is the pivotal time of truth; when the life you had chosen has evolved into something else, and its clothing and garments have expired like month-old yoghurt.

There are many winning points with following the Italian way of pruning a wardrobe down to the essentials; those pieces that belong to your present you, all fall under the folder called, investment dressing. You may have heard the terminology, and it may sound intimidating and a bit imposing, like a mother recommending her children to save money instead of splurging it on clothing. It's called investment dressing because it's intended to curate a collection of the classics or essentials, like the perfect white t-shirt or the straight pant.

Building your closet like a Lego castle becomes a reality when you treat each building block with respect and dedication. Take your wardrobe as seriously as Rome took itself, since we all know all too well that it wasn't built in a day. Before going through the juicy details, I want you to take a step back, and for a moment, leave aside lists, tips, suggestions and shopping, and put your lifestyle at the center, like a crackling bonfire ready for s'mores.

How many is too many? People say ten, some say 33 (don't ask, it's a formula). Honestly, even dealing with small armoire and limited spaces, the mindful, minimalist Marie Kondo's ideal ten-piece wardrobe is not anywhere close to what an Italian girl will ever get her mind around to. Now, between you and me, whoever is able to make do with ten pieces per season, has my respect and admiration. I am not even sure I can accept the challenge for a season.

The Italian and the American in me have never been able to edit that drastically; the reasonable shrinkage I have achieved, without driving myself crazy, ranges between 30 to 40 pieces per season, plus the evergreens and excluding shoes. My father always said I wasn't born to survive in a deserted island. A quantity that may be scary minimal if you kick off from an overflowing closet, but not when you consider that the total items one truly wears in a usual week don't exceed or differ much from it.

The idea is to have fun and enjoy the process as an all-encompassing exercise that wraps all aspects of your life. Why should you fight with yourself because you'd like to add both the white booties and the fedora? Why do we need to choose between the silk pussy-bow blouse and the Breton stripe t-shirt? We need our leisure time as much as we do work. Honestly, even when we think of the perfect camel coat or the white cotton summer dress, each of us has one in mind, and I can assure you they are all different. Even our favorites in our life have been different. My favorite right after I got divorced, was a piece of a collaboration of the then-rising designer Jason Wu with GAP. It was an A-line voluminous crisp cotton halter sleeveless mini dress that had lots of details like rouched collar and pockets, and it was perfect for the mini version of me, since at that time I was the tiniest size I have ever been. My favorite now is a linen deep plunge V-neck tea-length dress, because those ten years difference show in the knees, especially when you don't exercise. It's a dress I bought last summer during my last trip to Italy, from a small family-owned brand that only sells either in their garage or at the

"A lot of people have taste,
but they don't have the daring to be creative"
– Bill Cunningham

famous street market in Forte dei Marmi - the Palm Beach of the Italian Riviera. They deserve a small digression, because the mom-and-pop cute shacks or small neighborhood boutiques are what trains the eye to find those garments made with love, those not advertised or massively distributed. In truth, every female member of my family clan has owned more than one piece from this market booth, and one summer in high school, I even worked with them for pocket money.

Back to this 'basics' business.

The essentials are not the boring stuff even if they are the white blouse or the black trousers, they exist as foundation of a wardrobe where the main subject is YOU; the way you grew up, the way you live now, and how you blend them to be comfortable and appropriate to your current lifestyle. The imagination, creativity and morning inspiration are the gear to make them more than just boring basics, in turn making them unrecognizable, because that's the difference between you wearing your clothes, and the clothing wearing you.

There you have it. Know not to expect the 'top ten list' or any title-bait content that fills the web these days. But just because we don't follow the rules, doesn't mean everyone who finishes this book will get the radical rebel graduation diploma. There's plenty for everyone. Sit back, get an espresso or a Prosecco since it's got to be 5 p.m. somewhere, because you will have enough fashion to feel comfortable and proceed at your own pace.

A curated closet is not about minimalism or *maximalism* (as the new wave of Romanticism, started by the new star creative director of Gucci, Alessandro Michele, has been defined); it is about something close to a predisposition to seeking quality versus quantity. It is required to have some patience, research, and have the true longing to look good, elegant and intelligent at all times.

The truth is, there is only one Carrie Bradshaw with a wardrobe that exceeds her acquisition power by tenfold, and with an agenda worth the life of three busy city women. The goal is to nail down the 30 pieces you should invest on, the ones that you don't go cheap on. Not to make the rest of this paragraph a grocery list, I gave it an unusual twist, like a rhyming poem of several stances, one connected to the other. At the end, you will look good, straight-up good, like a mature and modern gentlewoman.

And the classics you want are: the crisp white blouse, a pair of black pumps, ballerinas, the flat thong sandals, the cashmere sweater, the right pants, a white T, the leather biker jacket, a pencil skirt, a camel coat, a pair of sneakers, the perfect purse. I am already thinking of one to five extra versions of each item. So you see the point, if you find the white T-shirt that fits your body contour to perfection, you'll want to buy it also in grey and black, and there the 10 pieces are gone.

When I think of the white blouse, it's Gianfranco Ferré that comes to mind; architect by education and fashion designer by trade, who carved himself a spot in history for creativity and exquisite taste. His designs made the 'white shirt' such an iconic garment, and they landed themselves museum status in Prato - the industrial province famous for its textile mills and its century-old tradition transmitted from generation to generation. What better home than The Textile Museum for a permanent exhibition of Mr. Ferré archives? Back to reality, this is what I mean by Italian style; you start form the stars, draw inspiration, aim high, and then find a compromise between astronomic prices and everyday life. There is a white shirt for every occasion, from the fitted button-down in boyish oxford material, to the tuxedo; from the white crisp must-be-worn-impeccably-pressed à la Carolina Herrera, to the one worn by your boyfriend the night before and stolen to have breakfast on the balcony.

The shoe: don't go cheap with the shoe. It'll hurt, look inexpensive and not chic, you'll walk funny, or after an hour will have to go barefoot (and not everyone can pull off a shoeless Armani gown like Julia Roberts at Cannes). The heel or flat dilemma keeps me failing at choosing because even after two decades in Miami, the reign of plexi heels, I tend to float equally. Here is where my major weakness lies: what's in a heel that a flat can't do? If I was to find myself in an emergency and could only choose one, I would crash, burn, explode, while going down with a pair of ballerinas and a classic T-strap, because you never know. The cognac leather flat thong sandal, made to measure ideally, is what keeps resolving your doubts, whether it's a day at the beach or a floor-length evening dress (watch as a reference, the last couple of Valentino Couture Summer collections).

Marianna Cimini, the Italian designer that lately became one of the 111 creatives included in an exhibition at the Triennale in Milan called, Il *Nuovo Vocabolario Della Moda Italiana* (The New Dictionary of Italian Fashion), which is based on the new generation of designers; the ones of the internet who represent the new fashion language.

Is sexy in the heel? Or will a pair of brogues do, if played well?
MC – "Brogues all my life, maybe to pair with a pristine white man shirt. I dislike being sexy in an expected way."

The cashmere sweater is a must, even at the tropics; Keep an eye on it, snap it while on sale at the end of the season, and it'll bring you way ahead when surviving through a summer dinner al fresco by the breeze of the ocean, instead of facing a colder-than-usual day with a cheap version. Don't do cheap. Be smart and be occasion-ready when the time comes. There is always the other option of borrowing that grey cardigan from the boys. It doesn't involve stealing, but you need to have a partner, brother or a friend like Leopoldo who, unlike Leopoldo, doesn't keep his wardrobe under the golden cupola like a dog with its bone.

The pant, if it were for me, would be wide leg, mid-rise with a couple of pleats, and a rolled-up unfinished hem and car shoes, but if you are more of an Emmanuelle Alt or Giorgia Tordini type of gal, you'll go for the straight peg cut pant, which in Italian we call, *cigarette*. Definitely, black is the color you'd want to go with, but how about khaki or grey wool?

The tee, the perfect white short-sleeve T-shirt, a James Dean, and here I pause and don't care aging myself with pride, because I am sorry, but I dare you to find anyone sexier than him in a white T-shirt. When you find your ideal one that clings on the body, enhances your endowments and doesn't expose the excess, you'll maybe want to stock-up on the crew neck, the V-neck, and then a long-sleeved one in all the basic colors: white, off-white, grey and black.

A biker leather jacket is a must-have piece, as well as a pencil skirt. These look best when you couple them with a pair of black pumps.

Have you ever dreamed of the camel coat? That enveloping long belted coat that makes you warm and fuzzy, and yearn for a cold winter weekend to be spent in the countryside in front of the fireplace, or in the woods searching for porcini mushrooms.

Everyone should own a pair of sneakers, and I mean for physical activity: running, jogging or a relaxed weekend at the beach. In an Italian closet, they either belong to the gym bag or they stay in their box and are used randomly. Nonetheless handy, "because you never know when the occasion arises", like my nonna says. And I'll leave it at this for now, but I will find the occasion to dig more into the theory of why 'Italians don't wear sneakers'.

The bag is another tough decision. They say you are either a bag girl or a shoe girl. I know for a fact I belong to the latter. But overall, the choice of the one bag is personal; 'someone may be more inclined to a spacious Mary Poppins style, while the other may cut to the chase and opt for a smaller crossbody or handle purse. It doesn't have to be designer, the all-over logo flashing, all it has to do is be of quality and serve its intended purpose. Choosing has never been my forte, as a matter of fact, the more I look for the perfect black satchel, the more I find that dark brown weekender scored years ago at a Hugo Boss sample sale; the perfect one that fits with every outfit for days at a time. The truth is, the pure Italian way steers away from the 'it' purse; the one shipped to all the influencers and pushed to sell before it even hits the floors, is and must be of no interest at all.

To celebrate people's passion for handbags, I want you to meet Sabine Masi of *Raison d'Etre* who has brought poetry into my world of handbags, or maybe the raison d'être that was missing. Her bags have that quality of looking worn and distressed, obtained through skilled hands of Italian artisans, and they tend to have a personality of their own.

How much research and trial is there before reaching the perfect nonchalant point of understated elegance?
SM – "There's only one research, the one to reach the harmony of the form. I'm referring to a cit. from Bruno Munari, the great Italian designer and illustrator.

Complicating is easy, simplifying is difficult. Only few are capable of simplifying. […] Eliminating instead of adding means recognizing the essence of things and communicating it in its essential core. – Bruno Munari"

Was it by traveling the world that an all-Italian brand was born?
SM – "It's always been a forever love; that passion I have always read through the eyes of the Florentine artisans when as a teenager I used to visit their workshops. My cousin used to take me in the '80s, he was the buyer for my cousin's leather goods store. Knowing the art of hand sewing vacchetta leather and creating objects saturated with that heart-warming smell of leather."

The bags are rigorously 'Made in Italy', which became its distinctive seal of approval. Was that essential to the birth of the brand?
SM – "It's essential, as an unmistakable imprinting; 'Made in Italy' has a precise characteristic. The idea can begin in faraway countries, but manufacturing it in Italy completes the circle."

Your bags are like a Mary Poppins duffel bag, where objects and stories live freely. They are born as hollow carriers of the mood of the day; they take the shape of one's character or philosophy. Do you grow attached to them?

SM – "A woman unveils her personality in each purse she owns. It's her own secret socket, and God forbid someone tries to break in and snoop around."

Could a bag be like the portrait of Oscar Wilde whose painter couldn't detach from them?
SM – "I must confess that at times it happens that, I too, don't have that exact bag I need for an occasion. It's like having them all at home. Truth is, I don't have that many."

You say that 'beauty will save the world' because beauty is overrated?
SM – "For each one of us, beauty is different. For me, beauty can be represented by vivid colors, for others simplicity can represent beauty, but for everybody, good manners and being good to others, is beauty. That's why I believe beauty will save the world."

When you design a collection or a bag, do you have a woman in mind?
SM – "She is a determined woman, positive, confident within her own skin and that brightens a room when she enters it. She's not fearful of dreaming, daring and leaving a mark behind. She is a woman that inspires me and transports me to create. Then there is Intractable - the unisex line dyed with an effect called, 'mestizo'. They are first deep dyed, dried

"I have never met a leopard print I didn't like"
– Diana Vreeland

33

and consequently overlaid with an ombré technique to be finally waxed. They end up looking vintage, used, that's why I chose to call it intractable.

If you have noticed some celebrity missing, you got it right. What I count as the 'Royalty of the Closet' - the blazer, the jeans, the Little Black Dress and lingerie - occupy a special throne on Mount Olympus. They are not overlooked; they just deserve a better space.

A quintessential "absolute" list doesn't really exist, in spite of how much the magazines and the internet try to convince you of the opposite, stereotype us within the racks, and homologate us behind cookie-cutter spreads.

Some random numbers to give you some direction, and help you choose the Italian way:

1. How many blazers should one own? Classic and tailored two-buttons, cropped, deconstructed, navy, tweed, black and velvet, strictly sartorial, and for the lucky ones, made-to-measure is the answer.
2. The height of the pant cuff: In the early '90s we were talking about five inches - exaggerated and temperamental. However, usually a good three-inch cuff like those in The Untouchables is sublime enough.
3. Pleats or no pleats? When confronted by the choice, always opt for pleats with discretion. A full midi pleated skirt could almost be a closet basic, even when the Gucci golden pleated skirt of the first woman collection designed by Alessandro Michele is a long-gone memory.
4. Hose or thin tights? Polka dot and lace tights, are they nerdy collegiate or The Graduate? It's all a matter of perspective.
5. What does it take for a complete summer vacation suitcase? Four bikinis and one bathing suit, two straw hats, three pareos, one floor-length slip dress, three slip-dresses/nightgowns, one pair of leather strappy sandals and one flat bejeweled sandals. What not to pack: tank tops, shorts, flip flops, visor and sport sunglasses, a 90 SPF white chalky protection, or you'll be looked at as l'americana; they will make you soluble coffee and charge you double for a scoop of ice cream.

"Your closet must be impeccably organized," people say to me all the time. You may wonder the same after reading thus far. The reply to that is: at the beginning of the season, yes! But by the end, chaos reigns with no shame. The truth is, I have fun when I get dressed, and as I don't follow rules,

Start from the Essentials

I never put things back where they belong. One day I may decide that instead of color coordinating, I want to start hanging more than folding, and half of the things get moved, but then I get bored in the process and don't finish, leaving behind something that doesn't quite look like closet heaven. I understand my own mess, the same way I normally have three to four started books in several corners of the house, because depending on the mood, I read one instead of the other.

FOUR

SWITCH WARDROBES SEASONALLY

Because there's nothing more annoying than wearing the wrong season, like linen or a bright turquoise chiffon blouse in winter, even at the tropics. Flash news: There's no such thing as one wardrobe for all seasons. This applies even if you live in a tropical climate and you think there's no room or necessity for winter gear. I have got news for you: the perfect gentlewoman adapts to the ritual of switching wardrobes.

Back in Italy, spring comes and its warmer temperatures call for opening windows, removing the duvet from the bed, switching the heater off, veering towards pastels, polka dots, navy and white, geranium reds and indulging in the short season of asparagus and wild strawberries. Life goes on with the seasons rolling out their specials, whether it's produce or fabrics.

Is your closet stuffed and overflowing? I have no shame to confess that mine became so when I moved to Miami. Now after years, I blame it on the "walk-in closet syndrome"- the effect by which the enthusiasm of being able to walk barefoot through your shoes and clothes, trumps shopping budgets and any sense of restriction. In Italy we have armoires, they look romantic, just imagine something out of the book *Under the Tuscan Sun*. Space is limited, what we do with them is nothing short of a miracle. Because there is no room for exaggeration, no matter how much you hang, fold or hide under the bed, you are obliged to move the season that is not in season, up to a less reachable section, which houses that *inganno* - the trick to also hide what we don't want to see or part from.

With the engine ignited, keep the momentum, and follow suit with the next three operations: Assess, Eliminate and Buy. You'll begin the trip to neatness in many areas of your life, think of 'divide and conquer', and act accordingly.

Roll up those sleeves and let's go hands in the ground.

When is it time to switch?

Depending when Easter lands, it's customary to take advantage of the short work week and proceed with the switch. The latest deadline is something very Italian – anywhere between Independence Day (April 25) and Labor Day in Europe (May 1). Only if you live in colder northern

Italy, from Tuscany down South, by that same date you have already indulged in the summer Dolce Vita for a good month or two. Fall makes the transition a bit easier, since back-to-school in middle of September, irrevocably puts the summer in lethargy with sadness.

As noteworthy as the reasons just mentioned, there is that impellent sense of renewal, the longing for sweater season and foliage, or for navy and white polka dots and violets. The fashion cycle is almost bipolar, and you start seeing spring clothing in the windows during January and February, when the season is at the peak of its polar schizophrenia. Whether or not you breathe and live fashion like I do, if you live in any of the fashion capitals like Paris, Milan or New York, you may have noticed the incongruence of ethereal, colorful, beach and summery vibes in the windows right after New Year's and sweaters, furs and tweeds in September.

Those are the months when designers show their new collections for the following season. February is the month to present the upcoming fall, and September next year's summer. That's the period, twice a year, when the fashion caravan, buyers, editors, stylists, media moguls, Hollywood guests, brand ambassadors and bloggers, hover around town for appointments and shows. There's no better time for stores to showcase the novelty and kick start the beginning of the season.

I live in Miami where there is no fashion week or noticeable seasons, except those two days a year when temperatures fall down to 70 F. So if you don't live anywhere close to a fashion capital, why do you still need to switch clothes? It's a form of self-love and appropriateness, rejuvenate the shelves, change colors, adapt to the temperatures, discover new combinations and outfits from the same clothes, and be ready to face the first spring rain showers, as well as the first fall rain with style.

Talking about the absence of seasons - something that hurts me as much as finding my car scratched in the parking lot without a note from the person who did it - are the shenanigans that accompany a dreaded cold front in Miami, where any temperature below 70 degrees is a felony. It involves a general aroma of moth balls mixed with freshly brewed coffee in the office; open-toed shoes, because "my toes hurt with any closed shoes"; it means lunch time at the mall to grab whatever-color fleece is left on sale, then worn over the silky blouse "because who cares anyways, it's only for a couple of days", until the building realizes it's time to crank the AC temp higher. I have lived through all of the above and realized that practicality is the problem that lies underneath. This creates an overall lack of luster, style and appropriateness.

Same works for the boot. This is a tricky one because why not have a knee-high riding boot, but how about a thigh-high mid-heel stretch suede? They are both highly impractical in Miami, except for those three days a year, but the principle remains the same. A wardrobe curated and assessed the Italian way, foresees situations, because a worldly gentlewoman is always ready to pack for a business trip, a surprise weekend gateway, as well as to face a sudden change in temperature. Not that my friends living in North Dakota or Wisconsin are exempt from the phenomenon, but when they come to visit Florida in the middle of their brutal winter, they all have their summer gear.

Why? What's behind the switching of the closets?

Granted, in Italy the primary reason is logistics, because bedrooms don't have walk-in closets and space is cut-out and used to the last centimeter. The bedroom is adorned with wooden armoires, often made to measure and built to cover the whole wall, from floor to ceiling, usually split in two levels - the lower more handy and easily reachable on a daily basis without need of ladders is dedicated to the current season, and the upper section is where the retiring garments go into lethargy. If there's no upstairs and downstairs, the 'off season' may end up in the studio or the guest bedroom, but it goes out of sight, retired with mothballs. If the family has a house in the mountains or one at the beach, the season-related gear remains there, until you grow out of it and it's time to buy new one because you wore it until it dropped dead, or just got bored of it and gave it to your cousins.

"I approach age with ice cream and a martini"
– Jenna Lyons

Absence creates desire, and after forgetting that gorgeous Valentino sleeveless black dress for a few months, you fall in love with it again, and remember once again the reasoning behind all the pennies you invested in it. 'No Whites After Labor Day', is an aged saying that still holds some meaning because you can still wear whites in the winter, but they are not sundresses or linen garbs. In Italy, we say something of the sort, 'No White Before Palm Sunday', which prompts everyone to show off a white or pastel outfit for Palm Sunday. The concept is similar though, the new season brings the happiness of change and the desire for a freshened image. If you live in a seasonless region like the Caribbean or around the Equator, the effort of switching seasons needs some more imagination and familiarity with fabric weights and runway novelty.

If you are like me and thinking of looking at the same clothing for 12 months at a time creates asphyxiation and depression, open a bottle of Prosecco, make a hot lavender bath to commiserate, and let the closet swap reinvigorate your adrenaline stash. Think of how much you save by alternating what you own already; Every six months the closet looks like a new store, new colors, garments, shoes, materials and accessories with an investment of a weekend, a visit to the seamstress for some mending, and the cobbler for leather goods.

How.

We go through three phases: You assess, you eliminate, and you buy.

It works wonders, true as a heart attack. You must imagine your closet as a reflection of your lifecycle, there's no summer without spring, there is no law school without a junior associate in a law firm and the partnership calls for blazer-power. A curated wardrobe is like a well-weeded garden; you take care of it even when the grass is frosted, but come the season, it beats the neighbors with splendor.

In switching wardrobes, the stage where you assess is as paramount as when choosing your wardrobe essentials. If there are items that you don't understand what possessed you to buy and wear them, now it's the time to let go. Whether it's the season that is temporarily retiring or the one coming to surface, there are goods worth definitive retirement or elimination, without sugar coating.

Lean from the balcony, and look at yourself as if you were a passerby if you want the process to take a smooth turn for sake of neutrality in the good direction. For optimal results, do it with someone, a friend, a personal stylist, a closet organizer, daughter, partner, or someone who has the best interest in you, while keeping a neutral stance. To hear that those distressed denim mini-skirts have no business anymore in your closet, can cause struggle, irritation and provoke a sudden sense of instability, the same signs you should be ready to expect when the change is about to happen. Having a companion amidst the misery will make an impact, and prompt results such as giving up those mini-skirts. You alone, would most probably make an attempt to find a billion reasons why you should keep them, and assessment would remain superficial and produce small moves of no particular significance.

The phase of assessing is brutal; I am not going to sugar coat it. It implies coming face to face with the raw you; Embrace it, and feel happy about who you'll find. Sometimes we forget how to have fun and play like a girl. You'll find quite surprising that most of the times when you are unhappy with what you wear or how you look, is not your fault; There's nothing wrong with you. You are just facing the wrong closet, the same one that was good for the old you. This is the pivotal moment when you know you are ready to proceed to phase two, the elimination.

Elimination can happen in various forms: donations to a charity, a foster center, a rehabilitation institution, consignment, and re-sell in the form of an auction site like *Ebay* or in luxury re-sale websites like *The Real Real* or *Vestiaire Collective*, if you own designer items. The most entertaining and engaging of all practices is the exchange where with a 'closet party' with your close friends, your garbage becomes somebody else's treasure. When they go in the hands of good friends or acquaintances, you lift from your shoulders the despair that you'll never see those pants again, and your sustainable conscience will be at peace that they didn't end up accumulated in a deadly polluting landfill. You also proceed to accelerate bonding and closeness with your friends, I can't tell you how many times I have heard and luckily said: "I have always wanted that".

While at it, you'll proceed blindfolded at times. You'll have no clue as where to start or how to finish; you'll feel sorry for yourself when there's no way back, all the clothes on the floor. To understand the attitude you need to survive your cleansing appointment, go back to those denim skirts and the feeling of anger mixed with desperation that surpasses even the simplest case of separation anxiety. Stop, inhale, take in the momentum, and keep it high until a good seventy percent of the closet is gone. The poor misfits will be piled up ready to reach various destinations, and we'll get at it in due time. At this stage, success lies in determination. The more you purge, the more your confidence level grows. Cleansing becomes therapeutic and lasting, when it builds on the belief that you are not destroying, but morphing into a new lifestyle. From a hurricane aftermath type of scenario, buying will be regenerating, fulfilling, controlled and happy.

You must be ready to live through the transition; it's emotional and can peak to moments of disenchantment. Reason why the presence of someone of certain pertinence in your life is highly recommended. Regardless of your level of expertise, whether you are a preemie or a veteran, those piles of clothes, accoutrements, empty hangers, will be teasing and tempting you to put them back in. No matter how much you try to conceal them in bags, even some of those bags will make no sense; they will be all excuses to keep in disguise, creepy and devilish undercover cops that will make you feel secure if you keep them instead of giving them away. For a few days they will be your worst nightmare, and when you hallucinate to think they become alive like in the movie, A Night at the Museum, you are on the road to recovery.

If you are not a beginner, you'll 'move like Jagger'. The selection will be tight enough to keep the majority of the clothes, mend and restore your investment pieces to better conditions, reinvent some outfits, and highlight the empty spots that need replenishing. Let the buying commence. If your role in the household, at work, or your life, has changed from the season before, you will look at your old clothes with a different set of eyes, which will cause a deeper cleanse, some extra investing, a spurt of resourcefulness to transform pieces. I have cut skirts out of dresses; divided a sequin mermaid dress into a top and skirt, and split them with a friend; matched an old distressed leather belt with a vintage silver buckle; recycled wool yarn from a scarf I had knitted and never worn, in order to make a new beanie; accessorized gemstone necklaces with scrap fabric from a man shirt (my ex-husband still doesn't know, it had been destroyed by the dry cleaners anyways). Here's when, in pure Italian style, the phone of your seamstress comes in handy and becomes a commodity. As for knitting, I thought it was boring and for the elderly, so kept fighting with my mom's persistence that a woman has to know how to knit, sew and embroider.

The Italian way wants you to leave no stone unturned and accomplish what Livia Firth and Eco-Age - the consulting firm she founded - have helped promote as the #30wears, because statistics show that an item of clothing is worn an average of seven times. Usually because it's cheap and made of poor quality materials, in conditions far from human, and defeating any sustainability principles. Said item is of insignificant value, bought mostly on a spur-of-the-moment trend plunge, not even worth mending because it would cost more than its original retail price, has a short shelf life and an equally short wear life. Chances are it gets tossed, because when used more than five to ten times it is not even worth giving away as donation. However, its life cycle will be endless, because the materials it's made with are not biodegradable, therefore will pollute a landfill somewhere in the world long after being disposed. Slow fashion helps you to be respectful towards the planet and considerate towards future generations. It stimulates creativity and self-esteem, and reduces carbon footprint. All of these benefits by simply adapting to the cycle of the seasons.

There are items that organically adapt to all seasons like silk and chiffon, some taffeta and cashmere, the king of the kings, depending on the amount of threads; it's always that chic go-to that makes it an essential for a last minute trip to the Caribbean or to the mountains. Because, as a matter of fact, you're a worldly woman always ready for a change of scenery and season.

And finally you get to buy - the happy phase. Don't we all love shopping?

You will be up for a surprise. As a matter of fact, you'll notice that after such a deep and thorough cleaning process, buying will never be the same. You'll approach the experience with a whole new perspective. This is the revolutionary, yet most rooted and ingrained aspect of the Italian way; Purchasing will have a different mindful meaning. E-commerce made things easy, a couple of clicks and no interaction with anyone, mostly done at night with a pint of ice cream next to you (c'mon don't be shy, I can picture myself in every single sofa I have owned). Truth is, we should say "enough with it". It's not that modern a

"People that take fashion seriously are idiots."
– Joan Rivers

concept anymore, and it has caused more damage than one can think of or we have been told.

I have assisted, virtually, to a salon discussion on *Items: is Fashion Modern?*, organized by MoMA and Paola Antonelli, its Senior Curator of Architecture and Design. It was a two-day event during which 26 iconic items, events, and accessories of the fashion world have been analyzed and shown their contribution to our lives in the 20th century. E-commerce was one of them. It made things easy, alluring so many to indulging and binge shopping, so much that on average we own 300% more clothes than our past generation, but we only wear things an average of seven times before we dispose. E-commerce has caused a domino effect that will lead to no good for our children's generations if we don't take action, follow suit and act to stop it. Fashion became the second most polluting industry on the planet because of the invasion of fast-fashion chains whose system is set to make money, not preserve Earth.

If you sit on the other end of the rainbow, and instead of looking forward to getting dressed, you don't really care about fashion and clothing. If you have adapted to the rhythm of a certain imposed work wear during the week, and jeans or shorts and a T-shirt during the weekend, I definitely need to inject some zest in that closet. Because that's not what an Italian style aficionado would do.

By now, I have spoken to many women, some have agreed to be featured in my blog too, and realized that what I went through is common; it's just that I had the strength to face it, and the tools to overcome the obstacles while keeping my head and style high. My reviews were enthusiastic and I hadn't compromised my style, because you can achieve numbers even when you care for wearing a duchesse full skirt from Oscar de la Renta instead of another ill-fitting, anonymous and banal black pant suit.

No matter the industry, lifestyle, upkeep, community involvement or the stage of professional growth, getting dressed is what we do; the fastest language. If you let yourself be guided by male-centered rules adapted to become uniform for convenience, you end up living in a false sense of equality.

To lighten up such a deep conversation that goes beyond the scope of the book, I have searched for the best of the best to talk about wardrobes. No matter how much incongruent people insist that her life and wardrobe are with the income she brings home, Carrie Bradshaw's closet is still everything in my imagination. I never tire of watching her evolution with the times. The series started in the '90s, and although her professional career always remained constant, she published a book and got close to getting married one too many times, but her wardrobe evolved in an exemplary way, at least in my imagination. A few years back, I had the honor of working in a photo shoot with one of the stylists from the *Sex and the City* movie, Danny Santiago, and he agreed to talk clothes with me. Danny is another of those treasures like Barbara Hulanicki, who we have the honor to have in Miami, and he has a pedigree in styling that spans from Vogue Italia to Elle, from Interview to Harper's Bazaar, working with celebrities of the caliber of Prince, Madonna and lately Iri Apfel. He is a glam whisperer; he walks into a room like a panther, soft and silent, but always damn dapper, stylish and ahead of the game. Give him a rack of clothes and a floor of shoes, and magic happens, glamorous magic.

You have a legendary collection of vintage clothes, accessories and decor: how did it start?
DS – "My fascination for vintage started in high school when I started visiting thrift stores and buying 1940s men suits to wear. Through the years I edited them, adapted them, making short pants, deconstructing them in Japanese style. Soon, friends started asking me to find them dresses for occasions; it was still a hobby then. Those were the times when I became more familiar with designers and styles, and during college is when I started archiving.

[NOTE: when he's talking about 'archive' he means museum-like archiving, pure collector style; something that if you haven't been exposed to before, you feel like a kid in a china store. Everything shines and you are attracted, but you remember your mom telling you: "no matter what happens, don't touch anything." He has pieces that make you drool.)

Does swapping wardrobes with the seasons help curate your style?
DS – "Absolutely. You change the seasons; first you take good care of what you have, you are cautious of what you buy, you don't splurge in trends, buy great pieces and pass them on from season to season, and then you interpret them in different ways. There are core styles that remain, but you refresh them; just think of a scarf, it can make a whole new look without anyone noticing."

I guess that's how you suggest to keep it chic at all times?
DS – "Keep it real."

What works best: spontaneity or planning?

DS – "Hard to choose, but as a stylist I go with spontaneity - the spur of the moment. I get one dress and go with the flow instead of confining into a definition; the story comes out alone. It's the same when you get dressed: depending on the mood of the day, one time it's minimalism the other it is not.

What's most important to complete an outfit: accessories or makeup?

DS – "With accessories, you can seriously express yourself. Makeup must be an accent, it must never be too much or overdone. When you have beautiful skin, you don't need to go strong on makeup, and it should never be the focal point."

What's in Italian style that conquers the hearts?

DS – "Romance. Think of Dolce & Gabbana, Gianfranco Ferré, Sofia Loren - it is seduction, but in a romantic way."

FIVE

IT'S NOT ABOUT THE MONEY

It wasn't difficult in the Magic City, with *Miami Vice* still fresh and on reruns, Versace alive and lavishing in his Ocean Drive adobe, Madonna *living la vida loca* at the Delano. Hence, the temptation of buying, buying, buying for the sake of showing that I was up to par with my Milan and my Florence; It was uncontrollable, not positive. Not being able to afford retail prices amped up by ridiculous import duties, spoiled by my previous life in which I had sample sales available 24/7; the road to fast-fashion and knock-off was rapid. The real me didn't want any of that and was hiding oblivious behind the shield of trying too hard, now I know it should have been the moment to stand by my Italian roots and focus on doing the best with less. Meanwhile, I kept buying, blinded by a fragile satisfaction that if I looked like the cover of the magazines, I would then be validated. By whom and for what? Those are still unclear. I became a lethal cocktail - a wannabe fashionista while in Miami, and an outsider while in Italy - where I would arrive with five suitcases for a two-week stay, and on the receiving end of sneering looks from people asking themselves: "what is she thinking?"

Glad it is over.

Nothing is unachievable now, but that in order to be considered a bearer of good taste you have to indulge in endless consumption - is a contradiction in terms. There is no need to overspend. Looking good and being well-dressed, is a balance of taste and brains.

There is no worst faux pas than pretending to be someone you are not. It's enough to learn a little lesson from the aristocrats. I don't want this to sound toff (posh or snobbish), but I have a theory to help you get closer to the idea that 'luxury is a state of mind where money comes after'.

Members of noble ranks inherit a privileged code of dressing from centuries past, and adopt it with reverence and pride. Their belonging to a privileged echelon of society is defined by a hereditary status that positions them on a higher pedestal. With their manners, language, attitude, distinct way of dressing, they speak a silent language; an unspoken Morse code that reveals itself only if you pay close attention. In truth, if you are not born into aristocracy, you may spend your life oblivious to how incisive their style is, yet imperceptible to the eye of the beholder.

The Cheat Sheet of Italian Style

I am not suggesting you binge on Downton Abbey ad mortem, what I am alluding to is that if you are aware of how to move like a noble, effortlessness will become your middle name. This is not a climb-the-social-ladder-race, it consists of getting into a frame of mind where you and your style are the same person, and you own it with attitude and entitlement. The saying 'wearing someone else's crest belongs to the footman', explains why trying to foul on your provenance and your economical means, acting as a nouveau riche, is pointless because you still remain a footman. Money and mindless spending can become a prison, and in the long run, a detriment to your self-esteem, since it can be humiliating to try and be a knock-off of someone else.

A privileged offspring of aristocratic descent doesn't follow trends, au contraire, and takes pride in wearing clothing with a till-death-do-us-part mindset. There's nothing more rewarding than cherishing and taking care of what's in your closet, because it makes it more precious, unique and personal. As per wearing logos or flaunting designer garbs, you must know the answer by now. Nobles have the same predisposition for their décor and gardens; the more disheveled and rationalized disorder, the more aristocratic patina. New is not the answer. Quality is what jumpstarts you to a mind of luxury. Seek for quality, not for a variety of mediocrity, because it will last to give you the highest ROI (Return on Investment).

Nonagenarian style maven, Iris Apfel, said in an interview: "Style has nothing to do with money; it's a matter of attitude. The most stylish people I ever saw were in Naples after the Second World War, they were really threadbare but put themselves together with such dash, like placing a flower in the buttonhole of a tattered suit." Naples is still one of the epicenters of Italian elegance; you walk the streets and feel passion, love, everything is colored vignette, the Med, the breeze, people take their simple dressing as serious as their coffees.

Luciano Barbera, style arbiter par excellence of man tailoring and heir to one of the top manufacturers of high-end textiles, says: "It's not how many clothes you have, but what you do with them." Having too many, clutters the physical space and the mind. When the ones you need are the good ones, you combine beauty with utility. You avert painless and delirious sessions in front of the mirror fighting with creases in the wrong place or too much fabric that deforms proportions. He says it and if you see him you become enchanted, as he seems to impersonate the word 'impeccable'. On the other hand, those painful long stares in the mirror where you know something is not right, I have had plenty. It requires patience, trial and error. Luxury resides in the mind when it revolves around quality not quantity; the only exception being time - the one element in your life that is luxurious when it abounds. As for the rest, it's a question of choices.

How to go 'for less is more'?

First, choose natural fibers and fabrics, they may seem expensive, but when you pay for research, tradition, heritage, you receive something of value that turns out to be timeless. When you pay for knock-offs or fast fashion, the calculation of what you receive is inverted, like being in a mortgage balloon payment - unpleasant at the touch, ill-fitting as the best of compliments, and with a life span shorter than a firework. All of the above will turn into step and repeat somewhere between five to eight wears down the road - dispose or throw away (waste, pollution), and buy again. That is the type of shopping you want to steer away from because it neither builds your wardrobe, nor reinforces your self-esteem.

It doesn't mean we have to go all custom-made, although dreaming is free and I never stop wishing, as should you. When in lack, the closest solution is buying off-the-rack and having a tailor fit every detail: hem, buttons and waist, all the features that make a difference between an ordinary outfit and a stunning one. Take a blazer for example, shoulders make it or break it, and they must hit your bone structure

"The greatest vulgarity is any imitation of youth and beauty"
– Diana Vreeland

49

so perfectly that no weird creases should appear around your shoulder blades. The buttons shouldn't pull, but close to perfection. Sleeves should end exactly where your wrist creases and your hand begins; they should proportionally blend with your body and make you look like you mean business. You should always wear the blazer, not allow the blazer to overwhelm your outfit or, worst, wear you. When none of the above happens, you look goofy and inappropriate, like a puppy wearing its harness for the very first time.

I am not preaching from the altar without a clue, I have gone through the process of being that puppy, oblivious I was one, and pretending I was somebody else. It was internal frustration that I hadn't realized was real; automatic response to the environment I had found myself in. I arrived to Miami Beach twenty years ago with the 'just married' sign and empty bottles rattling from the back of the red vintage Alfa Romeo convertible Duetto, which ten days before, my brother had driven me to church in. My status had now changed to 'married', but also to 'alien visa holder'. I had moved continents, and found myself living in a town where my (then) cultivated British accent was as alien to people around me as their Spanish was to me; my French wouldn't take me anywhere, and my newly acquired immigrant status wouldn't allow me to find a job unless someone was willing to sponsor me. This was a place where my background, education, experience, were as foreign as the stamp on my passport; Where habits, food, temperatures and way of dressing were as remote from mine as my wildest imagination could venture. In hindsight, I can read frustration all along, but back then it was denial and resentment that built up as a form of survival mode. All that was left for me to do was tell myself that I was going to show everybody who I was - from an imaginary platform of privilege on one hand, and my palms now filled with *arroz con frijoles* (rice and beans) on the other. I am using strong connotations, harsh brushes of color, because that was as deep as I was caught up in it; that is how it all resonates now that I have made peace with it. The catharsis didn't happen until many years later. Meanwhile, life went on with that inner voice of "you don't know where I come from", building up inside. There was no arrogance or meanness on the outside, my mama taught me well, to the point that I dipped in the world where I had to live in, learned to speak Spanish enough for it to become more prominent than my Italian, eventually found several job opportunities and got enveloped in the Miami way. Voila! Here I am writing about "the Italian way" via Miami, as much as it may seem contradictory, it's also an empowering path bringing it all out.

The "you don't know where I come from" was unknown to the majority of whom I interacted with, miles and centuries away. There was misconception. I was Italian but not the same kind of Italian as the ones whose ancestors, somewhere between grandparents and great grandparents, had emigrated and landed on Long Island or Caracas, Venezuela; I didn't know what Alfredo sauce was. And all I could find solace in was eating local, learning about this mix of American and the many other imported cultures and habits, and express it with my clothing.

The mechanism may or may not sound familiar. Change the factors, but the result is still the same; that pressure, now reinforced by social media, pressure of having to stand up to my standards. Mine was aspirational and behavioral. I needed to replicate 'my Milan' in Miami; the latest fashions, well-dressed people everywhere, glam, previous access to clothing that hadn't even hit the floors in a place where all of that was plain nonsense.

The Italian girl (in me) is somehow frugal and flattered like a peacock when she is complimented on a look that didn't cost her a penny. Same for when she doesn't have time to go home and change and buys drugstore makeup, the compensation is that she wears it with the same attitude as she would a total makeover at the Christian Dior counter. Don't expect full disclosure of the sources or any secret digs, much less if you want names and addresses, you'll most likely get something like: "Oh, I've had it forever and I would lie if I'd tell you where it's from". That is code for "Don't keep asking"; she knows exactly where, when and how, but you need to get into her circle of trust before she'll open up to you.

There are various options for being thrifty, a laborious and entertaining work that reaps rewards: buy local, go vintage and avoid sales without a purpose.

Same way that 'farm to table' has reached our plates and brought the way we eat back to savor seasonal produce and enjoy the flavors that nature offers without pesticides; with clothing it's a similar thought process. Look for what stands midway between designer clothing and high-street fashion, it's a world of possibilities, all you need to look for are well-made clothes, transparent sources, fair trade, sustainable materials, ethical principles, in other words, venture the slow fashion movement.

Simple? Not really. But feasible without a doubt, if you make a few tweaks in your normal shopping process. The internet and your local street markets are flourishing with brands, independent stores, self-made designers, mom and pop stores, many that may be sewing clothes out of their kitchen, but with love, inspiration, dedication and careful research.

Some of us are born with the natural gift of finding the four-leave clover in the garden, the rest of us must learn, counting on patience and acumen. You educate the eye to catch the unexpected, the needle in the haystack, the perfect scarf found in a hole-in-the-wall of frippery and sundries. You don't become a pro at a finger's snap, expect a few mishaps at first, some bad choices, but practice makes perfect, and when you get the hang of it you will surely land the deals. Educate your taste to the pleasure of searching, and then shopping will become entertaining and stimulating like it is for treasure hunters.

Since you are not falling for the sirens chanting of magazine ads or the fast-fashion impulse of charging those cards, you can focus on the proportions between utility and beauty. Let's say you are hunting for a pair of black pants, their beauty lies in the fact that they must fit you as if they were painted on; no camel toes to see, proper hemming, and the utility in how easy they are to upkeep, the use of natural fibers for a 'sophistication high' effect, and length in duration. The designer or the brand don't matter, discretion is a keyword that never goes out of trend. The value of them serving their purpose, combined with the beauty of their harmony, will result in them nonchalantly wrapping your legs without making an abnormally irregular string of sausages, or falling too short from the heel. The confidence boost makes it easy to keep your garments of choice at the minimum, so much so that in the morning you won't have to think much, your mood of the day will influence the choice.

You know you've scored when you receive a compliment. Rule of thumb: if the compliment comes from another woman, you've just scored double. That is when you realize it takes some time to look effortless, because you don't appear chic and elegant by buying the total look off the mannequin, or during a shopping brigade at the department store.

Vintage is another route to take. The possibilities of vintage stores range from consignment stores, street markets, Good Will (or any other similar organization), charitable pop-up auctions, estate auctions and garage sales. All of the above can produce the widest variety of feelings. I have friends that are horrified and disgusted by the idea of wearing belongings of unknown and, many times, deceased people. I suggest you take only the fun in. Breathe it in and out, do it like Mary Poppins, "a job well done has an element of fun". Keep an eye for that needle in the haystack, and know where the nearest ATM machine is because you never know. I have always perused antique markets and local street fairs since I was little, they provoke a certain adrenaline in me I call the 'hunting gear', which goes in reverse. When I look for something because I watched a movie or because it's my goal of the moment, I can never find it exactly how I have imagined it, but years later and when I don't think of it, it suddenly shows up. There are times I force myself to go shopping without the debit card and only a calculated cash budget. The Good Will Superstore is a great playground, especially when you find a pair of Ferragamo 'Vera' shoes at $20 that are a half a size smaller, but nothing the cobbler cannot fix.

If you are an online shopper type of gal, Ebay is huge. However, it can be as intimidating at times as Craigslist. It can feel like a jump into the unknown, no matter how many stars a seller has for rating, and if you look for brand-name goods, you never really have the certainty that you're buying authentic. Around the same wavelength of pre-owned clothing and accessories, there are selected sites that offer pre-loved certified designer items at a fraction of the original retail price. Places like *The Real Real* or *Vestiaire Co.* are not vintage outlets, they sell designer for less money, but the downside is that inventory is limited. Each visit is a question mark; consistency and determination are key.

Ever thought of renting wardrobe? This idea originated from wanting to make prom dresses and tuxedos available to young students, it later evolved into evening gowns during the 2008 recession period, and now it has expanded to simple daywear. It's a recipe that fits, as an example, the lifestyle of frequent travelers whose priorities don't reside in building a curated and

"Clothes make the man.
Naked people have little or no influence on society"
– Mark Twain

balanced wardrobe, but in keeping it fresh and always appropriate. The steps are straight forward: become a member for a yearly fee, access an extensive online inventory with an allotted sum to be spent monthly. The most evident perk is the liberty of traveling through different time zones and climates, formal and casual wear, you have the ability to flip through a huge variety of brands by size, color, look, inspiration, never be seen with the same outfit twice, all with a carry on. It needs perfect coordination with ordering on time to receive when needed, have time to try on and steam. You must know your agenda, and as a rule of thumb, prepare yourself ahead of time. Try on clothes from different brands and know how they fit your body, what size you are, so you avoid mishaps like having to wear a too-tight-to-breathe-in dress. I think it's a brilliant idea, maybe invented by someone who traveled a lot and lost luggage one too many times. I recognize how it would be the best option for one who goes for convenience first and is not interested in curating a personal wardrobe. My pace is more snail like, that is how I feel every time I pack for a trip and find that 'travel light' has never belonged in my vocabulary.

Last but not least, don't indulge in sales. Sales without a plan are a recipe for disaster, like going to the supermarket hungry, they appeal to people's FOMO (Fear of Missing Out) on a deal disguised in a 50 percent off plus a reward if you charge the purchase to the store's credit card. One more step towards debt hell. 'Sales with intention' is better alternative. This is a technique that requires the courage of the chase. You should try and aim at one great piece per season, let's say the classic khaki raincoat if you have a comfortable disposable income or are an ardent shopper. Go for one great piece per category, the drill is the same. Don't forget to smile. I have a real blast and I hope to transmit this through my words. I always find consolation in saying that fashion is my world. That magically sprinkled Narnia armoire that I want to see filled with gorgeous pieces is not filled yet, but those pieces that I have chased and snapped along the way, I cherish. Every time I wear them they give a star-dusted touch to my outfits. If all of this seems too much hard work, leave the task to a personal shopper or a friend who can keep an eye on things for you, and when the moment is right, can alert you that it's time to buy. I have done this for clients and we became good friends.

Curating the wardrobe, putting money aside for one piece at a time, and the pride of finally owning that great piece, will make you become jealous and protective of what you own and wear, and don't want others to look like a copycat of you. That is why I say and truly believe that "a moment cannot be mass produced". This concept of having style without swimming into temporary trends, means finding that signature style that suits you and encompasses age, lifestyle, social status, while offsetting peer pressure. The late Oscar de la Renta said: "Fashion is about dressing according to what's fashionable. Style is more about being yourself." Dressing up makes me feel awake, more present.

The Italian way begins with being cool with where you are, not keeping the best for last, and perpetually dreaming of that Prince Charming on the white horse, namely, that perfect camel coat. Still remaining distant from FOMO attitudes of wanting to be someone you are not.

I have talked about it with Federica and Pietro, the designer and creative mind behind the brand Asciari, a semi-couture collection made in Sicily.

Asciari is entirely handcrafted in Italy. Is the search for special and refined materials the beginning point of each new collection?
ASCIARI: "The inspirations for a new collection are originated from multiple and diverse sources: Italian elegance and tradition, personal style (shared by my mother and I), places and venues we travel to or even a special dish or fragrance. After that, we literally try to dress such inspirations by sourcing peculiar and hidden textiles. In this respect, only natural fibers (cotton, linen, silk, wool, cashmere, and alpaca) are chosen among the finest Italian, English and Japanese providers."

Do you suggest that the quest for the ideal wardrobe goes beyond clothing?
A – "The ideal wardrobe is a mirror of our personality, experiences, and certainly an expression of an esthetic and cultural path. In this respect, the ideal wardrobe goes beyond clothing and reveals the person, and specific attitude of a person towards different aspects of life."

How do you reconcile, if you do, with the pressure of the social media-driven habit of compulsive buying?
A – "Being proud of our Italian (or better said, Sicilian) heritage, we are not affected by mainstream and ephemeral trends. Devotion for sartorial excellence and luxury fabrics, combined with unconstructed cuts and minimalistic wide shapes, are the basis of our philosophy. The style is sophisticated, yet relaxed, very unique, personal and timeless. Our collections are made to last over the years, and therefore, across the hectic idea to be trendy. Of course, it does not mean that we live in a different era (or that we propose dresses for Edwardian times), but simply that we are in line with a more conscious "slow" way of living that focuses on authenticity. The ultimate sophistication is then 'less is more'".

If you were asked to build a wardrobe the Italian way, where would you begin?
A – "Pureness of lines combined with the finest Italian quality, which make a style effortless chic."

Is it true that Italians are always dressed up even to just go grocery shopping?
A – "Yes, I guess the fact that in general terms an Italian woman tries always to be in perfect condition regardless of the occasion or venue."

There must be some absolute NO in the Italian way. Is there?
A – "I guess socks with sandals and flip flops worn on any occasion different than by a swimming pool."

What would Leopoldo say?
L: "I owned Ferrari and Porsche in multiple units (This is true. Keep reading. It's not just a spoiled brat talking) before I was 25. I also owned a few speed-bikes, and I was never the type of person you'd expect coming out or off any of the above, because I was always myself, not a Ferrari owner. Now I am 33, I go to business meetings on a scooter, just wear my blazer, helmet and my older-than-me leather Tavecchi briefcase. It puts people at ease when you are not afraid to show who you are. Remember to add a blazer. Be daring. Express yourself. Tone it down a notch with a navy-blue blazer. Live life tastefully, find measure, be mildly inappropriate by means of true uniqueness, and respect others by being who you are."

SIX

BORROW FROM THE BOYS

While the fashion system is gearing towards genderless production and unified runways, there is something to be said about menswear and its impact on the development of modern tailoring. This is not a treatise on menswear and much less on womenswear, those you can find at a library near you, but there is a treat in the Italian way of wearing clothing that makes a woman want to steal from her man's wardrobe from time to time.

I started young, while goofing around in my grandfather's dress pants, which I eventually ended up wearing as a clown costume, cinched with a big belt and filled in the back with a pillow, to a town carnival. I could get away with everything except my nonno Bruno's ties, God bless his soul; I was his first granddaughter. I worked my privilege up through his side of the armoire that he shared with my grandmother in the master bedroom, for which I already had VIP passes.

My father's closet had more restrictions. I wasn't granted any favors for being the oldest daughter. He was always particular and jealous of his own wardrobe (in case you were wondering where I got it from). His number one coveted piece was a suede reindeer (don't judge, it was a thing back then) buttoned bomber in noisette - a tone darker than hazelnut brown. The jacket had a limited shelf life, it was unlined and too light for any temperatures colder than spring. Rainy days were out of the question. It was highly impractical, but glorious in every way. Only someone as neat and sleek as my father could be its perfect match. Besides, it was more of a male garment than a woman's, and I know how antiquated and incongruent that may sound in this era of genderless brands, but suffice it to say that the size was not even close to mine. Nevertheless, I was obsessed with it. I could only sneak it out of his armoire when it was a rainless day, which in spring is almost never, or when he wasn't traveling with it and I had my mother's complicity. There you have it, now he knows. And while I am at it, he might also want to know that the shiny croc black wallet that he always ignored, because according to him "it was too obnoxious", I used to shreds and still have it. Fixed by the cobbler and ready to be used to shreds for a good twenty more years.

I was fortunate to grow up surrounded by such magnificent examples of style, nothing of aristocratic origin, just genteel regular men, well-mannered and educated, who brought us up not with preaching lessons, but making us look up to them by their leading example, by naturally being themselves and telling us their war stories. Simple Italian living. I could name Cary Grant and James Dean, Benedict Cumberbatch or Brad Pitt, I should also mention Steve McQueen and Luchino Visconti; they all have style in common. They are almost mythical figures, some of them even have stylists on payroll that help them keep up with their preferred brand, and some were dandily inspired by their own choices of attire and genuinely interested in cultivating their appearance. Nonetheless, they feel pride and joy with being well-groomed and savants of what looks good on them and what doesn't, regardless of fashion or *quel-horreur* trends.

Because my ideal man is better than yours (of course everybody thinks the same thing), my job here is to first tell you who can't sit with us; the ones we are not borrowing from. I owe you a warning: I am going to depict some characters, the archetypes that I first perceived when I moved to the States. The reality is that I had never been exposed to any of them before, and chances are, if you are European, I'm pretty sure you have never seen your father sporting flip flops or your grandfather in a wife-beater *à la Italian mafia* movie. I am going to start with the list of these fashion villains, try to imagine them all lined up in the 'Most Wanted' wall at the police station.

'The Salesman', not the Don Draper from *Mad Men* though, more like *Matilda's* father, Harry, played by Danny De Vito. Those men who are bound to wearing a suit for certain attire requirements, and on whom the suit seems to have fallen on them like the wrong-sized lampshade you found at the garage sale. Those are the men that don't put any intention, thought, or goodwill into what they wear. Their only direction being that it ought to be a jacket and slacks, complemented by a clean shirt and possibly a tie, but completely oblivious of the proportions; where the shoulders should fall, when too much fabric is too much, where the sleeve should hit, etc. They are the ones that wear a blazer and look like *Mazinger Z* (you must be a kid of the '70s to know who this is, and have had brothers that forced you to play with its removable super powered arms). These are the same men that don't know that pants should gently fall with a slight break on top of the shoe, perhaps with a cuff, not be bunched up and dragged underneath the heel. Those same men who intentionally leave on the '100% Silk' label stitched outside the sport coat. On this last note, I have an anecdote.

My first time in New York, only three months into my new life in the U.S., I accompanied my then-husband to some bankers' dinner in a Mexican restaurant. Two things changed my existence ever since: being welcomed by a band of mariachis playing *la tarantella*, and this young Italo-

American broker wearing a 'Made in Italy' label sewn on the outside of his sport coat's sleeve. In Italy you don't hear la tarantella being played in the streets, and much less at your restaurant table, and the only place I had ever seen the label on the outside of a coat was inside a big outlet store, but never to be worn as a business card. It was an abrasive welcome; an eye-opener onto what the image of Italy was in people's collective imagination versus what it was for me in the movies. It's all a matter of culture and habits; in the end it was funny and entertaining. The lesson is that we don't take style lessons from that.

'The Silicon Valley' guy wears grey T-shirt, dad jeans and sneakers on repeat, which according to Wikipedia is "coolness that opts into sameness". It's really all just *normcore-* dressing in uniform, as obsessive and boring as metrosexual wear - that disappoints when it comes down to being inspiring in any way. Perhaps the only exception being, a Loro Piana cashmere hoodie. Remember luxury is a state of mind.

'The Sloppy' guy is the one who never really grew up and still wears his college T-shirts or sports team jersey with some amorphous jeans, sneakers, and white mid-ankle tubular socks. It's a look that I wish I could un-see alas. All I can do is ban it from my memory, wipe it off, and I suggest you do the same. A heads-up: if you find yourself frowning while bumping into such a representative of the frumpy hood in the street, blame it on me. There are no exceptions to this rule, not even if his name is Ashton Kutcher (he is taken anyways).

'The Stallion' is the guy who molds clothes around his chiseled body like Play-Doh. He flaunts his six-pack with a muscle shirt snug as a glove, preferably black, made of shiny stretchy material, usually found in the underwear department. Sometimes he is "avant garde" in his own genre and wears designer underwear and tees, let's say Versace, and shows off the label without thinking that there must be a reason it's found in the 'intimates' section of the store – he never gets the cue that it's meant to be kept private. To complete the look, the same dude wears slightly flared denim with embroidered back pockets and shredded by the heels of infamous unpolished black squared-point shoes. You usually become aware of his arrival by the cloud of his own cologne penetrating the air while he is still driving up the parking garage. Would it be warning enough if I'd tell you he is the unglamorous, uninspiring version of Tony Manero?

There you have a repertoire, some of the most common stereotypes enlivened by many variations of the theme, and you'd be shocked by the frequency of their occurrence. Just when you think you have seen enough, more creep out, like the aftershocks of an earthquake. I am far from questioning their integrity or shredding their persona to pieces; I am giving up my judgmental skills here. The presence of such a cultural and social mix in Miami Beach has immersed me in a reality in which the 'never judge a book by its cover' has been put to test with magnificent results.

I am more tolerant than the younger me, however, I am still the police of first impressions. I expect rules, gallantry, dignity, respect, elegance and codes to be enforced. Ignorance is not tolerated. I believe that a world of good-looking, dressed-to-the-nines people would be so much better. In an effort to make the world a better place, let's indulge in some good archetypes, the archetypal boys that own a wardrobe worth borrowing from. Just the thought gives me a sense of happiness.

I should first introduce you to *Sprezzatura*, Italian for 'studied carelessness' as defined in the Oxford English Dictionary. Originating from the Renaissance world of the arts and the courtesans, and it's meant to describe the apparent sense of casualness in accomplishing tasks that actually require hard work, skills and knowledge. It's the closest to the French word *nonchalance*, the avoidance of affectation typical of 'the Italian way', or steez listed by the Urban Dictionary as 'plain old style with eazzzz' and 'somebody's unique style'. It's what men like Gianni Agnelli and Lapo Elkan have done for generations, because they don't know better and

"Confidence is not 'They will like me', confidence is 'I'll be fine if they don't'"
– Anonymous

they are dead serious about it, like you would if you'd wear double-breasted blazers as your second skin. They are the men you see strolling at *Pitti Uomo* in Florence, the trade show for the men's collections that has *sprezzatura* written all over it. As a side note, if you are into boys, love Italy, history, art and fashion, Pitti is eye candy galore that everyone should experience once in a lifetime; it's bucket-list material.

'The Dandy': the name itself opens a Pandora's Box filled with Baudelaire, Beau Brummel, Lord Byron and Oscar Wilde; it's a way of thinking, a school of life and it's where I am heading to. A dandy is not a wallflower, he's the dapper, the dashing, the man with panache. He knows more than you, a man to whom you turn to when you don't know if you should leave your suede double-monk strap unbuckled. He takes his appearance seriously, he holds a responsibility, and if you ask him for guidance, he'll be flattered and somehow attracted to you, though he'll never admit it at once. (There are some traits of our Leopoldo in here.)

'The Minimalist', not the trendy hipster type, but the one who could be a trade man, a classic collegiate or the preppy eccentric guy. He is the best dressed in the room, good-looking is an understatement because by the time you have realized how stylish he is, he's already gone. When you happen to marry him, you scored not only a rare $2 coin, but an extra closet.

What would Leopoldo say?
L: "[Borrow from the boys] it's a little bit like women with short hair (short but not shaved): you got to show more femininity to borrow from the boys, but if you do it, it's sooo sexy."

Why borrow from the boys when as women we have enough designers and brands that our eyes can hold? It's all about wanting to be well-dressed and looking rakish, passion for tailoring, structure, lines and architectural construction, plus, nothing beats the allure of a man who knows how to put himself together. Because we wake up one day and feel like playing the vibe of a man role and wear brogues, and the following day we feel the need to tame the overly feminine chiffon frock with those same brogues. We are never bored and we take pleasure in getting dressed, we are not afraid of breaking the rules, and go genderless with flowing ease. Because fashion you imitate, but style you cultivate. Stealing some pieces here and there to interpret them with feminine touch only adds flair to this dance. Pair a school cardigan with a silk pussy-bow blouse and add a hand-army of signet and Victorian engagement rings, and it means that you not only know the rules, but also how to break them properly. One step ahead to your own signature style.

The Cheat Sheet of Italian Style

If the way a man dresses influences how a woman perceives him, the opposite is just as true. Italian women are attracted by a man who pays attention to what he wears, and in a passionate and enthusiastic way, no judgements or frivolity stamps. It is also true that an Italian man appreciates a woman who loves quality, heritage, sartorial details, and finds it intriguing to adapt the rigor to the fluidity of her body. It's like a game of rubber bands; you must balance yin and yang and perform a bit of the gamine game.

Borrowing from the boys is an investment in time where you automatically score the cool crown and walk a fascinating process. To bring you closer and make you more acquainted, I am going to give you one, the fine, relaxed yet effortless, Mr. Luciano Barbera, heir of one of the finest mills manufacturing luxury men's tailoring fabrics in the world. He has his own commandments, which I am of the opinion that they should be taught in school; if only schools were so cool as to prepare you for life and warn you that you never have a second chance to give a first impression.

Mr. Barbera is one of the most dashing examples of Italian style, born into refined low-key elegance, the one that doesn't get you noticed because of flashy elements, but remembered for being ineffable.

It's not a question of how much you spend on clothing, but what you do with it, which means invest your money with a purpose, or as Leopoldo would say: "No need to spend compulsively to look like a million dollars. Real Italian style is effortless and (please) has no brands or logos visible anywhere." Disclaimer: I advised you that he was going to be bold. Just imagine when you show him what you had in mind to wear and it's not of his liking. But I love Leo, and everyone should have one.

A man can never have too many white shirts. An apparent contradiction with what Barbera thinks about not having too many clothes, but he saves himself with the most romantic touch: at night a man is the frame of the beautiful woman next to him, so black suit and a white shirt is the way to go. Here is when the white shirt comes in as a blessing - the day after. It doesn't need to be tight-fitting to be sensual, we are not aiming at overtly sexy here, but if so, what's sexier to the eyes of a man, a sparkly bandage dress or his woman wearing his white shirt with stilettos? Food for thought: borrowing from the boys doesn't mean looking like a tomboy.

As per switching wardrobes with the seasons, it's normal for him to wear flannels and felt hats in the winter, and linen and straw Panama hats in the summer. This makes it easy for us, just go for the hat and good luck if you get caught. My grandfather's ties and my father's hats were off limits.

I wasn't even allowed to play dress-up with them; sacred material.

I was young and daring to dive in my father's closet, but that's how I built my character and style. Borrowing from the boys means being a bit of the alpha female (and if you are not, you'll reinforce the strings to become one). She is a good combination of charisma and determination. She doesn't accept "no" for an answer. She is confident and ambitious. She is intriguing and has her plan, whether a man is in it or not. She is loyal and trustworthy, and has no tolerance for lies. She needs to smile and have fun; no room for grouches or resentment. She is smart enough to forgive if it's worth it, or cut loose if it's not.

POWER DRESSING AND THE BLAZER.

Dress for Success- the book declared sartorial choices and shoulder-blazed power dressing, the winning formula to effectively get ahead in business. A few years later, Melanie Griffith taught us how to get dressed to mean "business" in the movie, *Working Girl*, while Richard Gere had us all salivating after his Armani suit in the movie, *American Gigolo*, which made him look like he was being illuminated by rays of sun penetrating through venetian blinds, and it can't get any more American than that. It's all in the blazer; the dignified, versatile, elegant garment, that from its beginnings of an army uniform has been adopted through the years and become part of regular wardrobes, even trickled down into women's wardrobes.

A blazer is a "passport for everything," says Luciano Barbera. Wearing a blazer means business and it simply puts to shame any discussion of the power there is in power dressing. We all know how our body language transforms when we wear a jacket, that's perhaps one of the reasons why Italian men always look well put together. We know that the patterns, cuts, and details of a man blazer can't properly fit a woman's body, but that a stunning blazer is a staple, is indeed a fact. As clever as physically stealing a jacket, so too is having the tailor be your best friend. Altering a blazer is a life-saver; it will rarely fit as a glove, but some creativity like throwing attention to the neckline with a chain or a scarf, rolling up the sleeves or belting it with a thick leather oversized belt, will do the trick. Chances are the material will be the scene stealer.

When looking for a seamstress, it's a good idea to also include tailors, because the secrets they know, the solutions they bring to the table for alterations or cutting, are worthy of another planet. If you have never done it before, it's never too late to borrow from the boys, not only their clothing, but also their experts.

Charlotte Rampling and *le tux*, and Bianca Jagger with her famous white pantsuit come to mind as iconic wearers of power dressing. A modern version of a pantsuit is a deconstructed jacket and a pair of culottes with lace-up stilettos; it goes from day to night, just change the drawstring sac to a small vintage clutch.

A SNEAKER AFFAIR

What's in a heel that a flat can't do? Here's where we talk about ballerinas (a Milanese style as true as the gold Madonna on top of the Duomo), flat sandals, penny loafers, desert boots, double-monk loafers and sneakers.

I have a personal story to share about sneakers that may explain why you barely see a typical Italian wearing them, with the only exception of the *Superga*. In my Italian way of growing up, *athleisure* - the trend where clothing designed for performing sports, is instead worn at work and in casual venues - was not yet a thing; sneakers and denim were code for male-worker gear. As discriminatory as it may seem in 2016, I grew up with the notion that 'denim is too cold for winter and too hot for summer', and 'American tourists wear sneakers' - reason why we don't wear them. In other words, if you were born one and a half generations ago, chances are that you owned your first pair of Nike sneakers as a high-school sophomore; mine were a pair of white Nikes with a hunter-green wing. Vintage dealings.

This idea in the second decade of the new century may seem unthinkable and outdated, but it puts to sleep trends like *normcore* and *hipster* for which the sneaker is a sole form of accessory to wear. The obsession with the brand or a particular style of the brand, is at the core both normcore and hipster, with opposite visual results. *Normcore* became all the rage a couple of years ago and to give you a glance, think of a mix between the late Steve Jobs and Jerry Seinfeld; a non-descriptive 'Silicon Valley meets Hartford, CT' way of putting together a fleece, mom jeans and sneakers. The term *normcore* was first born from the minds of a trend forecast group called K-Hole, and they successfully made it happen as a fashion trend. This trend is the anti-fashion, the opposite of the hipster- the precedent trend - whose sneakers, jeans, and sweaters methodically chosen and matched by color, style and textures, are as anal as they are eye-pleasing. With all that in mind, there are many Italian hipsters and not that many normcore aficionados, as you may imagine. However, those Adidas, New Balance, Birkenstock sliders and Dr. Scholl's, do exist in my own wardrobe and in that of many more Italians as a staple; something that's been bought for a sporty occasion, and it stays in that category, trends or not.

STYLE CONTAMINATION

Being "duded out" will produce a hybrid, which can put romanticism in a simple grey cashmere boyfriend cardigan or the fedora, which we used to call in Italian, *il Borsalino* - the felt medium-brimmed gentlemanly hat.

Women dress for themselves first. We look at the mirror and observe with our eyes, instead of wearing their shoes, we wear our stilettos with the pride of a peacock. The news is that, at least to an Italian man, the attraction for a woman who borrows from the boys is inexplicably natural. Since Italian style is not about being overtly sexy, but being sensual, by stealing his vest or wearing his chain watch, we acquire that intangible seal of femininity.

Brogues are classic, yet a woman in brogues, maybe splashed in gold, has its own charm that can become a spell for any man. Men are not necessarily attracted to a woman who lives constantly in heels. I can see some brows rising and I'll leave it at that, but I promise you will be noticing more women in brogues, wingtips, double-monk strap or tasseled loafers, especially in Europe, and it won't have a negative result.

"You can have a career and like clothes."
– Theresa May

65

Wear them with distressed denim shorts and a blazer over a white T-shirt, pair them up with a sleeveless plisse midi-dress and a cross body schoolboy bag. Don't forget to wear sunglasses.

Perfume: a sign of rebellion and the curiosity of cupping 'the prohibited fruit'. We all have a little Eve in us, which makes a bite of that apple too tempting to pass up. The chemistry of a body with less testosterone produces an unexpected skin reaction; perfumes are never the same on a man than they are on a woman.

The white shirt: think of that scene in the movie Pretty Woman and how her life changed by using Richard Gere's shirt the day after; it was romantic and cathartic.

Cardigan: that cozy romantic all-enveloping feel of being wrapped in a cashmere sweater, especially when his cologne is still on it.

GO BIG OR GO HOME

That is pants, bags and watches.

'Big pants don't care', could be the tagline. Coco Chanel was the first brilliant mind to use man tailoring for women. The jersey fabric and the big wide fluid pant; the unexpected. I am talking about a wide-leg pant, even a multi-pleated, oversized and exaggerated-leg man pant that makes a statement on its own, and if cinched at the waist with a long crocodile leather belt knotted at the front and worn with a T-shirt and a blazer, is power dressing par excellence. A ruffled top, a pair of killer stilettos, maybe the most feminine D'Orsay style will complete the look, and make you enough 'gamine' as Emma Watson or a modern-day Audrey Hepburn.

A-line pants: an evolution from the flat front and buttoned sailor pants, are another way to borrow from the guys and make it feminine. Unless you are already tall and lean, any of these types of pants call for a sexy heel, the thinner the heel the better. No platforms or flat-forms allowed, bulky would exaggerate volumes.

If you are daring enough (and if you are not by now you'll get kicked out of this game), grab those pleated linen trousers from your man's closet, wear a big belt, roll the hem up and add a gorgeous T-strap stiletto. If his size is too much of an issue for you, go to the men's section of your favorite store, J. Crew or Gap, and try on their chinos. You never know, but it could become your next obsession.

As for the bag, Italian women have one thing with bags - they are usually big. My taste for bags was shaped by three styles: my grandfather's briefcase (we call it the 24/7 impeccably polished), my aunt's medical bag that she used when she first started the profession as an on-call doctor, something we now only see in the movies, and a *Bagonghi* - a multi-colored velveteen Roberta di Camerino purse that is now hard to find even in real vintage stores. Two out of three were utilitarian, and the rest is history.

THE THEORY OF THE BIG WATCH

This is another one of those unspoken truths. It is almost always a reality that an Italian woman would rather wear a big watch, something up to 40 mm in diameter, and not a costume one, but a real watchmaker one like a Rolex or a Panerai. I have no real explanation to this preference, other than it feels good; it's a conversation starter. It means "boss" just like that power blazer does. It just looks good. I wouldn't read too much into it, except that sometimes having expensive taste other than for heels is a good thing. Of the multitude of brands I could have interviewed, I found one the most intriguing - Out Of Order (Damaged in Italy). This is the first brand of watches that are sold already scratched and distressed; luxury in the imperfection.

'Made in Italy' has its own aristocratic patina of quality and excellence, what are the values that a brand has to stand by to be successful in a global market arena?
OOO – "Well, the values that a brand has to stand by to be great in the world are obviously the quality of the manufacturing, and the passion that a customer breaths when he touches one of your products. Speaking honestly, I don't know if this rule is valid for each brand, but for sure it's what I want to transmit to the people. I want to give them an emotion, more than give them an easy object."

Your watches are cool and you are peacock-proud of them. Your products are said to be 'Damaged in Italy', how did you arrive to the extreme concept of making something so precise yet imperfect, as an already damaged watch?
OOO – "First of all, I want to say that I'm peacock-proud just when I see people happy and smiling in front of our products, they find the name of our brand very funny because it speaks by itself and doesn't need particular explanations. Well, I arrived at this result after a lot of research, and a huge

quantity of experiments and trials together with Mr. Dario Ceolotto and Mr. Claudio Dalla Mora and all our team, which without each of their own know-how nothing could exist today."

You need artful skills to achieve perfection, and a watch must be impeccably built or it won't serve its purpose. Why did you want to make it disruptive?
OOO – "Three years ago, when I started with this project, I wanted to change the rules; give something new to the people so they wouldn't have to worry about scratching their new watch, which usually happens after the first night out with friends. As I've already said, I love to see people happy and so I'm sure that a person who wears Out of Order, feels better; he takes his own day or his own free time more easily than before, and last but not least, he feels inimitable because each piece, thanks to the handcraft work, is unique and unrepeatable."

A woman wearing a big watch looks like she's borrowing from the boys, can anyone pull this off? Shall we launch a movement of the gentlewoman?
OOO – "We could say that each one of our products is thought to be unisex in order to satisfy each taste. Anyway, […] we have plans to please and amaze in the near future!"

What's the appeal of an OOO watch that a vintage one doesn't have?
OOO – "Simply, a vintage piece is something which you try to handle with care. An OOO watch already has written on its back case to 'treat it badly', so you don't have to worry to damage or scratch it. It has to not only tell time, but also tell a story."

Italian style in one or two words?
OOO – "Classy, different."

Is wearing your signature wrist watch the equivalent of having a signature fragrance or having something that can be passed down from generation to generation?
OOO – "Our collection is mainly ongoing. What we create has no time and yes, when one Out of Order is passed from father to son, we will surely have reached our desired result."

SEVEN

APPLY MAKEUP WITH DISCRETION;

NEVER LEAVE WITHOUT PERFUME

Choosing to wear little makeup has nothing to do with being Italian or feeling sexy. It consists of the same mix of convenience and simplicity that forms the foundation of effortless elegance, and goes beyond borders.

It is a given fact that, as a child, we all had a field trip in someone's makeup drawer at one point or another. I, for one, am guilty as charged. It is also true that it didn't have any damaging effect on our future relationship with men, because nobody should give makeup too much relevance. The habits you grow up with stick, even when your life takes you through different continents. By telling you my story, a pretty common Italian story, my intention is to give you another Polaroid for the scrapbook. At least now, whether you go barefaced or not on your next trip to Italy, you'll remember me before concluding that Italian women are not groomed.

Standards like simplicity, minimal effort, attention to details, prestigious products, quality, heritage and tradition, are the largest tassels to form a luxurious mind. To be clear, we don't live like Catholic nuns and give up any attempt of embellishment. We are not deprived of all that glitters, but we reach that phase later in life, almost when it can no longer be avoided. That's where the ritual of restoring the face at the last minute, and with minimal instruments, is rooted; at the point of no return, where decency and distinction call in and you must respond.

The first time I ever wore full-on makeup was for my 18th birthday party, same time I was allowed to buy my first pair of kitten heels. It was exciting. I felt like a debutante in Vienna. A lady from the beauty parlor came over to my house before the party and, in less than half an hour, I went from barely-of-age to looking twenty-seven. As a note of reference, in Europe we legally become of age at eighteen, which is also when we can get our driver's license and be considered 'mature', at least on paper.

I was one of the few girls left in the group that didn't wear makeup or heels. Most of them had already found their way to the only *profumeria* in town; an old fashioned family-owned version of Sephora. Not that I had unforgiving parents who would force me into austerity, I honestly just had little interest in all that. My mother has always been the type of gal to pull her gilded Helena Rubinstein red lipstick and black eyeliner out of her purse two minutes before having to face other people. At home, my father and younger brothers were all about boats, sailing instruments, clocks and geometry, so it goes without saying that a conversation about how to build a squirrel-welcoming treehouse was more probable, than one having to do with any kind of lip gloss lingo. Newspapers and magazines were only sold at the newsstand back then, and Sunday's ritual included a visit. Inevitably, my brothers would go for ones about cartoons or power boats, while I would choose a fashion magazine. Although they were expensive, my mom and I would both read them, so the ROI was unbeatable. I remember 'that' being the excuse while squeezing my copy onto the pile of things at checkout, under all the figurines, so that my dad would pay the total sum without itemizing.

I just described the inner workings of a typical Italian family, pretty standard stuff. As much as it may sound silly, anachronistic and suburban, it is exactly my point: the Italian way is simple and memory driven. How does slowing time relate to the choice of a red lipstick? By using more of your time to spend it with your children who excitedly prepare to go to their friend's birthday party, instead of spending it in front of your vanity or in the powder room lathering yourself in colors. It's no coincidence that vanity or powder rooms are not real-estate fixtures in Italy; the bathroom is. The bathroom is shared with a good amount of drama, which increases exponentially with the number of females versus males that live in the household.

Core concept is 'never try too hard'. No fuss or need of useless adornments for a theatrical or insincere version of yourself. 'Consume in moderation', could be the tagline; the same one that rules the choice of food, cars, and clothing the Italian way. We now live in what I'd dare call the "Kardashian effect" - I can't believe I even had to mention their name, but that's how much their popularity has sadly penetrated our American lives. The reality is that today we are bombarded by YouTube tutorials, bloggers and their endless list of DYIs of this and that, at all times. TV shows that prompt you to buy what will make you look like XYZ celebrity in the wee hours of the night. They have democratized the once inaccessible, sometimes prohibitive, market of beauty products, and the choice is yours. Similar to fast fashion or slow fashion, it's a matter of abundance versus frugality, consumption versus parsimony, and it starts with the little things, like an eye liner.

Be confident of who you are, spend that extra minute looking at yourself in the mirror, and appreciate your features and flaws. Embrace them because they make you who you are. No strobing or lip-enhancing tricks will boost your self-esteem more than being your true self. Less is more, as banal and déjà vu as it may sound, which works wonders when deciding how much makeup is too much makeup. When you think you have already fully prepped and groomed, take that eye shadow a notch down, and elevate your attitude. Fully own the brightness of your pupils and be intentional about how you present yourself, this will surely land you that contract, dinner date, a smile from your daughter (that looks like yours) or a kiss from your partner.

Talking about relationships, the good news is that Italian men are not attracted by the 'makeup on steroids' look. They are more intrigued by a challenging conversation, and with finding out who is behind that girl of few words and solid education; one who doesn't try to impress them by putting forward a Bambi face or strip of fake eyelashes. Even more exciting news, this same man will be the one who when you wake up the next day, will kiss your pillow face, puffy under eyes and bed hair; no dreadful surprises. The man who loves you will love you even more, having been conquered by your radiating confidence.

"Fashion is the armor to survive the reality of everyday life."
– Bill Cunningham

The Cheat Sheet of Italian Style

How should we carry a glowing and makeup-free face?

Keep it natural and take good care of yourself, says the one who used to fry under the sun in the highest peak of heat while lathering herself with damaging bronzing oils instead of SPF. I am lucky, genetically and geriatrically speaking, that I don't look like a cracked terracotta tile. I was born and raised in a seaside resort town where, come March, all you'd think about was leaving school to suntan. We'd head to the beach so early in the morning that the umbrellas and beach clubs weren't open yet. Then came the time when wrinkles, freckles, and aging spots were all having a feast on my neckline and face. That was the moment I had to learn about collagen stimulation, exfoliation and proper hydration. Back in my youth days, I was happily reckless. I was not thinking then, that twenty years down the road, I would be dealing with the inevitable law of gravity. A cruel law that loves playing a game of 'the higher your age, the lower your skin hangs'. All that, compounded by the fact that Italians speak with their hands and a plethora of unfiltered facial expressions. No 'resting bitch face' for us, sometimes it's all in an eyebrow.

Regardless of rights of birth or age, a solid skin regimen reduces the time you'll spend in makeup application, which comes in handy in the unfortunate walk-of-shame event of having your under eye bags and mascara blend in unison.

Cleansing, exfoliating, hydrating and protecting, are four crucial steps you should perform daily like a sacred dance and never leave home without. I have a dermatologist, because in Florida it's almost as mandatory as having air conditioning, but I don't have an aesthetician (*l'estetista* in Italian). When I feel I want a massage, a deep-peel facial, a dermabrasion session, a silver foil mask or any of the exotic concoctions that make you look as fresh as an English rose, I ask around, look for coupons online, and get the 'best of the best' at that moment. With the passing years, I spend more time on my morning and night routines than I used to, but when I see my skin glow, the rosy cheeks and barely-there pores, I feel younger and proud; proud like when my daughter became the Chief Photography Editor of her school's art book.

Besides a rigorous skincare routine of cleansing oils, milks or soaps (I don't rely only on makeup-removing wipes, unless I am not at home for the night), I also resort to Retin-A (that is the prescription version of Tretinoin 0,50%), vitamin C and E, hyaluronic acid, magic potions for those pasty black under eye circles, meditation sessions and inner conversations with my "11 lines" - the spot in between my brows that makes me look like a grumpy old version of myself - and the right nutrition. This last one being paramount. All that goes down the esophagus cannot be expelled, it manifests itself again on your face, almost like karma, a "did you really have to eat that pizza at 11 p.m.?" type of karma. I may have black under eye circles and you may have puffy under eye bags. I may have crow's feet around my eyes and you may have a double chin. I may have a Mediterranean diet ingrained in my pores and you may follow a Scandinavian diet. Regardless of these differences, adequate morning and night routines are your best friends. First, take the time to look at yourself in the mirror for a few minutes, with your heart and conscience in hand, just you and your face, not in a hasty no-time-to-put-on-makeup type of mirror session, but a good ten-minute one-on-one-love mirror session that makes a tremendous effect on your self-esteem. Second, you scout out all the places that carry the creams and potions to address your personal flaws, and those makeup products that will help dissimulate said flaws each morning. Third, after you have performed your sacred routines for a good three weeks, you'll start noticing results; an inner endorphin-fueled glow will begin to show, accelerating rejuvenating effects.

What happens if you do the no-makeup diet? I feel the huge responsibility and honor of convincing you, the right way, of how liberating and empowering it is when you let your facial features free to stand on their own. But you must wear some makeup; those pesky under eye circles and law of gravity, must not be left unattended. The difference is that instead of this makeup application taking place in the powder room for (what seems like) endless hours, causing fights with your significant other and arriving to that children's party after the candles have already been blown out, it happens in the elevator, the train or the car, preferably at the traffic light.

One other thing that is never missing from any Italian woman's beauty bag is a Labello lip balm – the blue and white cap is as truly Italian as it gets.

A friend, makeup artist and creator of a line of cosmetic products, once told me: "When we are young we want our face to be matte, and all we desire is to hide the glow and shine. As we get older, all we look for is the glow of a plump young skin." This now makes me think twice every time I am faced with choosing a particular foundation or primer. It has made me be more grounded about my age; it has defined the best type of foundations for my makeup ritual, still confining them to the intermittence of the traffic light and all fitting in one pouch. The way to go is 'as natural as possible', staying close to your true self; tweaking your flaws a bit so as to highlight your best features, but being careful of not going 'Lady Gaga' on it.

Trick is: understated and naturally minimal makeup. A perfectly executed 'no-makeup makeup' look consisting of foundation, mascara, lip gloss, a little blush, a sparingly bit of concealer, eyeliner, lip liner, and your best Kung Fu moves to make eyebrows look on point. The ultimate goal is to achieve the "I woke up like this" face by minimizing signs of aging and marks left behind by a fulfilling life, in a subtle, almost invisible manner. The good thing is that everything under the sun is available with the use of a credit card and cosmetic stratagem like primer, finishing powder, highlighting sets and color correctors. To get the red carpet treatment, turn to a red lipstick and a dramatic smoky eye, just remember to not rub your eyes during the event or you'll end up with awful raccoon eyes, which happens when you are not used to it.

One recommendation, because I am as passionate for Italian style as I am for our planet Earth, please try to be a conscientious buyer. Spend extra time doing some research, use that free Google for a good cause, and read the labels. Go beyond the allure of that magazine ad, don't bet all your chips on a marketing promise of what that product will supposedly make you look like, instead, make an educated choice. Choose to respect the environment, and refuse to wear any man-made chemical-riddled concoctions invented to speed up production timelines regardless of human conditions or animal welfare. I'll leave it at that; the final choice is yours.

The second part of this chapter's title almost quotes Marilyn Monroe - who was said to only wear a few drops of Chanel No. 5 to bed. Your own perfume is as vital to the Italian way of style, as drinking coffee in the morning.

For as long as I can remember, my great-grandmother smelled as fresh as her Violetta di Parma essence, while my father was proud of his own British cologne because he felt it brought him closer to that English countryside aristocratic lifestyle he kept channeling. Smelling the aroma of freshly-brewed coffee in the morning is a relief for the rest of the day. The smell of freesias marks for me the beginning of spring, the same way a perfume is reminiscent of a moment - nostalgic, happy, fearful - unique to everyone. My daughter thinks that *Acqua di Rose* by Johnson and Johnson, which I make her use as a toner for her face, "smells like old people". How that came to be in her mind, she cannot explain; my concern was to make sure that I wasn't the "old people" she was thinking about.

A scent owns a multisensorial power that goes beyond the smell and drives it back to the brain. In other words, we take the choice of a perfume seriously. The perfume industry is worth billions, and for this part of the project we aim to tackle the upper echelon of fine fragrance, not the synthetic by-products. We are goddesses after all, and we don't buy perfume at the cosmetic counter after being treacherously spritzed for a few reasons: One of them is, we are not like anybody else. It wouldn't hurt to remember to wear our invisible crown and a bit of snob appeal when fragrance shopping. An extract that has been diluted in solvents creates an artificial moment of uniformity for the sole purpose of marketing and sales. This is when the 'we don't follow trends' affirmation goes into full gear. We want a story, a narrative, an illusion; a promise to travel back to a safe place where we feel queenly. It all has to happen with one pump in the morning that will last for the rest of the day.

The art of fragrance is older than fashion and clothing; it goes back to ancient Greece and the worship of gods through offerings of the essences extracted from tree saps and roots. Perfume is a luxury experience that transcends the triviality of being stuck in traffic or in the movie theater line, and transports you to a higher level. Perfume is an attitude; it speaks of you. That extra pinch of snob appeal is what makes you be remembered every time that your scent is around.

The search for your own perfume is intimate and personal. Perfume tackles a special mood; a moment of the day when the light is striking just right, and it blends with your skin. In other words, when a friend gifts you with the latest perfume sold at the cosmetic counter for your birthday, you know there is no real friendship there. Chances are it may have been comped as a gift with purchase.

The search for your signature perfume may be long and expensive. It's like looking for the perfect truffle or expecting the perfect storm. It should go with the seasons, therefore there should not be just one perfume in your repertoire, but several. I learned this lesson by falling in love with the line called, Arquiste. I am fascinated by how its founder, Carlos Huber, confines a historical event into each scent. A story in a bottle is what my fragrance was for me. I used to be so Italian that I would only wear Patchouli by Reminiscence; that's actually how our conversation started, and a whole new world expanded from there. My story before Arquiste: Patchouli was the perfume I had chosen or perhaps that had chosen me, when I first moved to Milan, accepted my first job after college, and broke up with my boyfriend. It was a seal of comfort, determination, freedom, independence, and sadness that I didn't want to give up even upon moving to Miami. Not even if it meant I couldn't find it anywhere except for the Fiorucci store in NYC. That was the one item I would buy, as soon as I landed back in Milan, at the mythical *profumeria* Mazzolari in Piazza San Babila. That fragrance stuck it out with me through thick and thin. This is how my friendship with Huber started, by challenging him to convince me that Patchouli wasn't my signature perfume after all. Little that I know that my daughter and I would become so enchanted with the world of fine fragrances, which aligns perfectly with the Italian way of luxury living as a state of mind.

Carlos is one of a handful of refined noses in the world of fragrance; if you ask him he will dismiss it due to humbleness, but it's the truth. He is more than just a fragrance developer. We had a conversation where we talked history, we went from Florence and the Mediterranean to Mexico City; unexpected topics when you think you are going to be delving into technical fragrance talk -first notes, second notes, alcohol content, packaging. Now, sit back and prepare to be introduced to the power of fine fragrance.

Warning: if you find yourself with the sudden urge to get rid of all the perfume bottles lined up in your vanity, it means you got bitten by the bug. Embrace it, don't fight it, and consume in moderation.

Each of your fragrances refers to a historical event and encapsulates the olfactory references related to it - art and history, research and discovery. A spritz of it brings modern life back through centuries of civilization and cultures. Would you say it's the ultimate form of portable luxury?
CH – "I certainly think it's a huge pleasure. Fragrance goes beyond a luxury good or a beauty product, it is storytelling! As you mention, with each Arquiste scent I want to tell you a story that inspires you. In turn, a fragrance created with this much attention to detail will say so much more about you when you wear it; it will inspire new stories, speak of your style and taste, your own background and

"A woman that doesn't wear perfume has no future."
– Coco Chanel

76

interests. It shows, you have an appreciation of scent as an art form. So I would say stylistically, it's the ultimate form of expression."

Your fragrances speak to both men and women, most of the events they are reminiscent of involved a great deal of both. Is the distinction of perfumes for men and women an old marketing trick in an era of genderless fashion?

CH – "Gender in perfume has generally been associated with marketing. It was (and still is in the mass sector) a way to identify the potential user, and streamline your marketing efforts to pitch it in the most effective way. Needless to say, for the luxury goods consumer, the 'pitch' has to be completely different; what that person wants is to experience the brand or the product by him or herself, not to be pushed or be confused with the obvious. The stylish customer also has an appreciation for beauty and quality that goes beyond gender, so in the niche fragrance world, it's better to let people choose for themselves what they will want based on their own personal taste or desire. However, this doesn't mean that gender is erased, and you can still propose more feminine or masculine fragrances. This still gives personality and color to the fragrances. There are certain fragrance notes that act as code and are meant to help people understand the fragrances' personality, if you will. For example, a sweet floral note will be interpreted as more feminine, where as an aromatic rosemary note will be traditionally perceived as more masculine. But these are just learned habits, by no means, are they exclusive or reductive of gender. I believe the most important thing is to try a fragrance on your skin and see how it smells ON YOU. Your own skin and chemistry is very important in determining how it smells. It's all about what makes you feel good."

An Italian girl applies little makeup, but never leaves the house without wearing her fragrance. Is this another form of defining her own style?

CH – "Fragrance is one of the most distinctive references of style. To define your style through scent, to manifest your personality in a way that is both subtle and unique, is a really beautiful thing. It completes the real life experience of how you define yourself and choose to present yourself to the world. You can own a perfume bottle, but your heart owns what's inside."

Can you compare synthetic perfumes and fine fragrances to fast fashion and slow fashion?

CH – "No, it has nothing to do with that. First of all, synthetic notes are not necessarily the enemy of fine fragrance. In fact, the reason why fine fragrance is what it is today is because of the technological advancement of 'hyper naturals'. Secondly, because the quality, attention, and time that a fragrance developer and a perfumer can spend creating a fragrance has nothing to do with their choice of natural or synthetic ingredients. The issue in fragrance is quality. You can have magnificent high-quality synthetic materials and terrible ones. The same with naturals. You can have the most noble, rich, natural ingredients or the most flat, unsustainable or low-quality ones. The choice is to use ingredients that are multi-dimensional, that are filled with nuances, that are conflict-free, as green as possible, and that offer the richest olfactory experience."

When we first met, I was an ambassador of my own signature perfume. You taught me how a woman is not solely defined by one aspect of her style. Can you elaborate more on that idea?
CH – "This is fragrance, not a marriage. It's an easy, attainable luxury, so you should have fun with it and vary your scents, whether from weekday to weekend or from one season to the next. With that said, think about your style not only in terms of the clothes you wear, but of the image, vibe, and attitude that you exude. You can change in and out of your clothes, but a scent has more depth. Choose one that draws you in. It will likely draw others in, too."

Think for a moment of being our guide in this itinerary to defining one's style: what's an absolute 'no' in choosing a fragrance?
CH – "Never buy something before smelling it on your own skin, and never underestimate the quality of a scent. Style in fragrance means quality ingredients, a well-blended scent, and certain elegance about it. You can be wearing the most stylish, elegant clothes, but if you smell cheap, it defeats the entire purpose. The same goes for the opposite. You can be in jeans and a t-shirt, but smell (and feel) like a million dollars. And that confidence is what makes you shine!"

EIGHT

BUT FIRST, SHOP IN YOUR CLOSET

One common misconception about Italian style is that it's an expensive hobby. Truthfully, I believe luxury is a state of mind. It begins in one's point of view and by now you are with me - the Italian way is an example of finery, understated elegance, simple and grounded. As for the 'effortless' aspect, I have bad news. What may look as effortless is not improvised. It's actually fruit of research and trials, but when you learn it, then it's just a matter of step and repeat.

Don't buy by impulse. This is a way of living that needs to be tackled via two different aspects: how to do it and what to buy. This is how you make your closet worth more than any shopping spree could ever buy you.

Mindless consumption and shopping sprees are not the Italian way, and again, my grandmother has a valid theory about it. When she'd see me coming back home for the summer from Miami, and buying *en masse* clothing, accessories, food (anything I could not find in Florida), she would candidly tell me: "You definitely didn't live through the war". The idea is not as dark as it seems at first glance, as she obviously survived World War II, gave birth to my mother while the family had been evacuated from the shores due to bombings, and my grandfather had been deported by the Germans. According to her, the Americans arrived with a new sense of opulence, plenty of produce, food, survival kits, yet she says they were welcomed with reserve. Pride and gratefulness were the mixed feelings that grandma says were circulating the streets at that time.

Living off a potato soup or a vegetable broth made with three old dried-up lettuce leaves and a wild onion, had become a daily endeavor. As well as, wearing any clothing one had until they were so worn out the collars and the hems had to be reversed. That idea that nothing could be trashed and everything had multiple uses, became ingrained in one's lifestyle; an essential and unspoken part of Italian lifestyle.

Find the signature style that suits (pun intended) your lifestyle and you'll overcome age and social status, if you live in an environment where such a thing is still 'a thing'.

By not taking yourself too seriously, like hopefully you have already learned to do, you'll feel at ease with where you are at. Keep perpetually dreaming of Prince Charming on that white horse, but remain undisturbed by FOMO, propelled attitudes of wanting to be someone that you are not. Simply, wear the glass slipper that nobody else has. There are only three ways to own a glass slipper: have it made out of imagination with a personal choice of fabric and finish by your personal tailor, find it in the granny's closet, or scout it out in a vintage store.

That doesn't mean you will look like a fish out of water at the British Embassy Christmas party, but that you'll acquire the habit of digging into your closet first to come out with a never-before-seen outfit; fruit of the mood of the moment, and the 'Royalty' pieces that now live in your wardrobe. How about, for said Christmas party, you choose a great simple tuxedo jacket (you never know what you could find in the attic) over a long slip-dress, and paired with sparkly stacked-heel booties.

Mix off-the-runway with older staples of your wardrobe. Be crafty, reinterpret a velvet cropped blazer (torero style) with a white T-shirt and a pair of distressed jeans.

Be a conscientious buyer and, foremost, a resourceful keeper. If you want to do it like a true Italian, when you have an event (birthday, wedding, etc.), don't go all deep into credit card debt to buy the whole outfit at the department store, instead, first reach out to your closet, as you would to your best friend, and pull any garment that you deem appropriate for the occasion. And here you must be careful to wear the same head-to-toe outfit you pulled together on another occasion, regardless of whether the same crowd will be in attendance or not. This is where a scarf, a fascinator, the family jewelry, a clutch, and a new pair of heels make all the difference.

To use a food analogy to describe how authenticity deepens its roots in simplicity - an Italian afternoon snack is comprised of a piece of bread topped with a slab of dark chocolate, or a sliced blood-orange with sugar and freshly-pressed olive oil. As alien and unusual as they may seem, do yourself a favor and try them both. You'll be blown away by the exquisite contrast of flavors. To prove my point, search your pantry with the mind of a pastry chef and you'll learn that to make a Pavlova - a more exotic-sounding concoction that it really is - all you need are simple basic ingredients, and the skills of looking behind the glaring glass of a seemingly empty-looking fridge.

With that in mind, the idea of ever buying an outfit for one night and returning it the following day will become unrealistic, and not even be considered in your wildest dreams. And the why is simple. All along, you were not being conscientious, resourceful; you spent money on some garments that you don't recognize yourself while in them, garments that don't have your style or character in them.

The smarter way to go is to not spend a dime, and pull from your own belongings for a more personal result that will receive unexpected compliments. When you have cleaned up your closet and replenished it with quality essentials, that A-line little black dress will always be your first and favorite bet; creativity is your next best ally. Add a turban, sparkly socks and open-toe heels and make it very quirky; add a short cape, lace-up brogues and a fedora and make it chic; wear a turtle neck underneath, an oversized knitted scarf, heavy cashmere knee-high tights and booties, throw a beanie and go for a Saturday morning stroll. The choice of opting for minimalism or 'more is better' remains a matter of personal decision. Italian style can go either way, it adapts and percolates through the cracks of your lifestyle.

The most recent story with my favorite little black dress has an intriguing beginning and the most revealing ending. Three years ago, I re-shared on my Tumblr an image by Scott Shuman, the creator of blog and social phenomenon called, *The Sartorialist*, and a photographer whose street-style I adore for its sensibility, simple elegance and creativity. The subject he chose was a girl from the back, crossing the street in what seems to be Milan, wearing flat sandals, a satchel, huge black curly mane and THAT dress; black with blue inserts made of what looks like crispy cotton, cut in

"Fashion is not something that exists in dresses only [...] Fashion has to do with ideas, the way we live."
– Coco Chanel

A-line with a nice V opening in the back. I fell in love with the image and the dress. That picture got a lot of 'likes' and hits on social media. Eventually, winter came and we all forgot about it. A year after, I met the photographer with his then-girlfriend at a book signing in Miami. I devoured his book and in the process of reading I found "the" picture, which made me proud in knowing I was right for liking it, but also reminded me of the dress that had caught my eye months before. A year later, I found myself in Milan, in the showroom of the very designer and subject of that infamous dress, Marianna Cimini. Besides finding out that she and Scott are good friends, I learned the story behind 'The Ballerina Dress' (that's how it's called), and how its top version was worn by Marion Cotillard at that year's Cannes Film Festival. I love the story, and adore how a friendship from the Mediterranean to the Atlantic was born based out of a passion for fashion, quality and dreaming.

The first interview I had with her will resonate with the fact that the secret of a well-curated closet, that houses the essentials, is poise, passion and tradition.

From being an intern at Max Mara to being chosen by Marion Cotillard, what drives you?
MC – "Common sense, courage and recklessness in equal portions."

What happened when you saw yourself in The Sartorialist? You know, that is where I discovered you first.
MC – "I have always followed The Sartorialist. So when, by coincidence, I bumped into Scott Schuman in Milan and then saw myself published, it was indeed fun and exciting. Coincidence wanted the dress I was wearing when photographed by him, to be one of the ones I am the closest to – 'The Ballerina Dress'. It later became a basic of every collection.

NOTE: Follow The Sartorialist (Scott Schuman is his name), and get your hands on a 'Ballerina Dress'.

What's the first piece you ever designed?
MC – "I love outerwear. They are my refuge in the winter; my passport when I travel. The first piece I ever designed and created completely by hand, was a coat made of 21 tweed inlays and a navy woolen double crepe. Matching everything to perfection was why I could call that a little big dare!

How much of your personal style is in your collection?
MC – "I never design anything that I wouldn't wear. I am always trying to create pieces that can be recognized, but without a cumbersome and overburdening personality. I structure the collection with different layers of interpretation, so that each client has freedom to personalize it according to their style and physique."

NOTE: Alber Elbaz says "if it's not wearable it's not fashion". Point taken.

What was the catalyst that started it all?
MC – "A profound devotion for this profession and a good dose of determination. Without those two elements, surviving and growing from one season to the other becomes impossible, since difficulties and obstacles, which an emerging brand encounters, are never-ending.

Is the quest for the little black dress boring or a challenge?
MC – "A marvelous challenge! The black dress is timeless, every woman should own at least one LBD in her wardrobe perfectly tailored and of impeccable fit. I haven't chosen the path of confrontation with the classics of fashion history. Let's just think for a second of the magnificent dress designed by Givenchy that Audrey Hepburn wore in Breakfast at Tiffany's. I have tried to draw a new route, all mine, in which I have tried to combine practicality with elegance, defying the element of time. That's how 'The Ballerina Dress' was born."

There's rigor and powerful femininity in your collections; what do you attribute that to?
MC – "Cleanness and minimalism is how I reach the essence of femininity; with no makeup or tricks!"

You became one of the chosen designers of the Vocabolario Della Moda Italiana; what does it mean to you, so young in your career?
MC – "Just being included in the selection of the designers that represent the future of Italian fashion and being at the Triennale, has been a surprise and a tremendous honor. When Paola Bertola and Vittorio Linfante, the curators, and I met for the first time, we immediately clicked in syntonic harmony, and we contaminated each other with equal enthusiasm. Then, when I saw my 'Goodbye Coat' displayed in an exhibition in a museum, it was surreal, to say the least."

The Cheat Sheet of Italian Style

I realize that having a grandmother's armoire filled with gems to indulge in, is pure luxury and one of those that must be cherished itself as a unique gem. By the way, grandma is still alive and "sprint" - like we called her that time she jumped across the barricades to take us under one special fountain in Tivoli, a town near Rome famous for its 1000 fountains. Her armoires and chest of drawers are still present and standing like little soldiers after so many years, and just as welcoming every time I go back to see them, as when I was ten.

Good news is that an in-case-of-emergency solution to replenish the absence of family heirlooms, is going vintage. As much as it strikes the wrong chord in me to realize that my childhood whereabouts are "vintage", or to put it like my daughter does "from the other century". Regardless, antique shopping and window shopping was one of my beloved family weekend activities; when the town's promenade or the neighboring medieval hamlets were closed to traffic, and transformed for one day by tables and booths filled with treasures. Books, custom jewelry, candelabras, paintings, maps, Navy paraphernalia (my father's is a family of sailors), watches, ceramics.

My grandfather was a collector of stamps for a while, at least until he discovered that we, his ten grandchildren, were not at all interested in such a tedious and meticulous endeavor. He then became a collector of a children's weekly magazine called *Il Corriere dei Piccoli*. My father's was a family of sailors, so travel mementos were the norm.

Flea markets and vintage stores became all the hype these last few years in the United States. Blame it on the advent of the hipster/millennials generation or the 2008 recession. Without dissecting the sociological and anthropological implications that factor behind the phenomenon, let's leverage on it and help you get one step closer to the Italian way. Miami Beach in its own manner of adapting to novelty that trickles down from big sisters New York City and Los Angeles, has built a relatively solid flea market crowd that gathers every other week on Lincoln Road during high season - October through May.

It brings me joy to take my daughter there and make her experience something as close as my real youth while growing up in the New Continent. I take pride in using slow living at its core as a definition of Italian style. Take time to smell the roses, drag, if necessary, your nose up from the phone screen and take time to savor your coffee or the quality of a fabric, all with the same intensity.

What should one find in a closet to make it a Pandora's Box the Italian way? What I refer to as "The Royalty", the closet essentials on steroids: the blazer, the perfect denim pants, impeccable underwear, a wide-brimmed fedora hat, an (eco) fur coat, a silk scarf, last but not least, the little black dress.

The little black dress: "… is not a style per se, it's a conceptual fashion […], it's modern, it changes, but it's always the same […] a kind of a chic armor," says Valerie Steele at MoMA's *Items: is Fashion Modern? – Abecedarium*. Black is mourning, elegant, chic, fashionable, punk, dark, economical, modern, sexy, alluring, day and night, simple, cocktail and every version of black dress each in a different fabric says something different with its wearer.

The blazer: The ideal is a tailored blazer that falls on your body like a general's uniform. Rigor, impeccable detailing, exquisite fabrics, buttons, shoulders, pockets, it's all the good stuff you can indulge in, in a made-to-measure suiting experience. I can't afford custom, and like me, all of us commoners living in a city that gained the nickname Magic City many decades ago due to its seemingly overnight growth, and where 60% of normal people's income goes into housing, a made-to-measure blazer would topple our budget and get us kicked out of the apartment for a good month. The closest solution to the divine life of the likes of Gary Cooper is off-the-rack and then a visit to the best tailor in town. An explosive combination, all behind the seams paraphernalia that will make you the most rakish guy or gal of the room, or the pool, if you are in Miami.

As for denim, I mean the unparalleled fascination for denim pants that at some point

"I think it's better to be happy than well dressed."
– Iris Apfel

85

in life touches us inevitably. I am talking about those jeans that fit you like a glove and work as your inner scale of comfort; that excite you or send you into despair, depending if they still fit or not. Denim could also be considered a luxury. It makes you feel at ease, comfortable and chic, with only a few occasions when it is not appropriate to wear - the courtroom, when you get married, and a black tie affair. In the collective imaginary, a good pair of jeans has a story, is raggedy, worn, lived in, authentic, nostalgic, daring and reassuring. Wearing a good pair of jeans should mean feeling at ease and comfortable like when going out for dinner with friends. The jeans are a premium choice, as well as are the quality of ingredients in the best pizza or who we choose to spend quality time with. It's a big and slow affair. Denim is the great equalizer, and, as the late Yves Saint Laurent has namely admitted: "[...] I wish I had invented blue jeans: the most spectacular, the most practical, the most relaxed and nonchalant. They have expression, modesty, sex appeal, simplicity."

Underwear (I prefer calling it, lingerie), is the foundation to every great outfit. It's the silent partner of a corporation. The fact that you don't see it, doesn't exonerate it from having to do a terrific job. The irony is that when it shows, it's actually doing a bad job. Lingerie is supposed to make you feel naked. After all, we live in it all day long. It's like being in a relationship; it's supposed to hold, lift, wrap you in just the perfect places, and the day something goes wrong is because the wire went haywire, the elastic lost its elasticity or, worst scenario, you have put on weight.

We choose lingerie based on a few concepts. Comfort and luxury, since after high school we no longer wear Fruit of the Loom packed undies or Pink by Victoria Secret cotton panties that feature smiley faces. Now we opt for lush and sensual, because we have to dress our sixth sense. It must tease, just imagine Mrs. Robinson in *The Graduate*, and the art of leaving something to the imagination; it doesn't have to scream 'sex'. You confide in them like you do your secret diary, they become your best accomplice and partner in crime, embellishing your form, favoring your femininity and boosting your confidence. With the right bra and underwear (rigorously matching, please) you don't hesitate wearing a silk see-through blouse or a pair of form-hugging pants, because you know that proportions will be respected and the law of gravity contradicted (you'll understand if you read this and are over 40).

We don't do cheap, you got it right. The above mentioned doesn't happen with a Mossimo lycra push-up bra from Target, or Victoria Secret for that matter, which is just another fast-fashion brand that only looks amazing on its "Angels". You want softness, enveloping lace, luxurious material like cotton and lycra, and believe it or not, bamboo fiber.

But First, Shop in your Closet

How many bras are there in a closet? There should be at least five strapless, the underwired regular in black, white and neutral, the *balconnet* lace and silk. Since we are talking intimates, I feel it's time I disclose the details of our relationship with these garments - it's complicated! We love, cherish, and meticulously care for our silken and lacey treasures. We wash them by hand, never tumble dry, tuck them softly into drawers that get their lining paper changed constantly, and every year we add an aromatic bag filled with new lavender from the garden. The same way we match our underwear to our bras and buy double panties per each bra, it's also true that we don't always wear a bra. We think of it as sensual without being vulgar, because if you do it without taking yourself too seriously, it comes across as natural instead of posy or sexy.

A felt wide-brimmed fedora, which in Italian we call, *Borsalino*, referring to one of the oldest and most renowned companies producing the highest quality of felt hats since the 19th century. How many types of hats and turbans must we count? A felt fedora, a cloche, a wide-brimmed straw hat. Turban is a bit eccentric. You must demonstrate a great deal of confidence to wear one without looking like you belong on the *I Love Lucy* set, but the silk squared Hermes (or any other) scarf is a must.

I mention fur, and I leave the choice between real fur and eco fur to each of you. I see no need to judge or take sides. Fur is glamorous, quirky, colorful and splendid; you can dress it down with flat boots (even rain boots), heavy tights and a boyfriend's cashmere hoodie, or dress it up with killer heels, naked legs and a slip-dress for the opera. From hipster to flapper.

About the silk scarf, I must mention that my grandmother Titti still now at 94 always wears one - summer or winter. She went a long way with hers, from grocery shopping to church or the theater. It was always a Gucci that I remember. I think for a sense of patriotism she would never sport a Hermes, not even when one of my aunts gave it to her one Christmas, in fact, she took it back in exchange for something else. According to her, it has (as she still sports it knotted along with her gold necklace and pearls) some inexplicable magic powers to keep you looking elegant and well put together, while also protecting you from the breeze and fierce winter winds. Truth is, she'd never get colds when we were kids. I'll just leave it at that. If you don't own one, don't buy knock-offs. You can easily find the original and most classic ones by Gucci, Ferragamo and Valentino for example, at the outlets. If the silk scarf is not really your thing, one pashmina, cashmere shawl or oversized scarf is the passport. Carry it everywhere, like Snoopy's blanket, wear it around the neck, hang it on your crossbody bag and keep handy in case the air conditioning is blasting and you get the chills at the movies. The scarf is a savior.

This topic is one of the most "you're so Italian you don't even know how much", if that even makes any sense. It's loaded with hues of slow living, cherishing belongings for their meaning and timeless quality that go beyond fashion. It implies taste, food, produce and somehow reinvigorates a style of living that was one in which abundance and materialism, spending and consumerism, were not included.

There is a constant connection between fashion and food, and that is style. In Italian we say: "tell me who you hang out with and I will tell you who you are". Taste is such a potent sense. You can have taste for the beautiful things, have an expensive taste, but you can also have a sophisticated palate that appreciates haute cuisine as much as modest peasant eats. Cashmere is the noblest of all the fibers, and your taste detects it for its qualities of softness, durability, warmth; Olive oil being its regal equivalent. It is still, after thousands of years, produced by manual harvests. The selection and mix of olives is cut down to science, the final product is a perfect blend of yin and yang, tart and sweet, comfort and coziness.

Alice Agnelli, from *A Gipsy in the Kitchen* - a blog that takes her around the world to know and talk about food - cooks and bakes dressed in sequins and her boyfriend's sweaters. She is the ideal personification of style and food. Coming from the fashion world, her last corporate job was PR officer for Stella McCartney for Italy and southern Europe, she now runs a blogging business. I am proud to count her as one of my great friends across the pond.

As busy as she is, from a trip to Sweden to a series of suppers that she organizes at her cozy abode with her boyfriend and their new family member, Brie the pup, we had a chance to exchange a sweet WhatsApp conversation.

"What's the link between style and food?"
AA – "The link is always love (heart Emoji ensued)"

"Did you grow with equal attraction for style and food, or one brought in the other?"
AA – "Style has always contaminated everything I have ever done. And when I talk about style, I refer to a modus vivendi, a way of living in which style is personal, random, led by the emotions and feelings of the very moment when I find myself selecting an outfit or a recipe. Sad? I go for a creamed soup, a crumble and a cashmere sweater. Happy? Then a great meringue with strawberries, a glass of good wine and a denim overall."

"You have a book, 'Le Ricette Dal Cuore' of recipes that filled your heart, what's your fondest?"
AA – "I can't really say what my favorite recipe is … each one has marked a special moment in my life that I can't choose one, I love them all, for one reason or another. I can tell you though, what I would love my children ask me for Christmas lunch: risotto with pumpkin and chestnuts, brandada de bacalao, string bean tarte and an apple and blackberry crumble."

NINE

THE DISRUPTIVE ELEMENT

There's something elusive in the Italian way, a *je ne sais quoi* that needs a whole book to define it. It cannot be described in one or two words; it's curiosity, observation, traveling, imagination, inspiration from the arts, museums, movies, theater and ballet all put together.

That which you would never expect makes a look personal, feminine and with character. Have you ever thought of wearing flat sandals with a floor-length red-carpet gown or a deconstructed blazer over a strappy lingerie lace dress? Simple garments become lavish when beautified with some extraordinary and unexpected embellishments. Combine feminine silhouettes with masculine and sartorial cuts.

How to put it together: when wearing a white lace dress, don't pair it with a parure of custom jewelry, strappy glitter sandals and a clutch, instead wear Beatles booties, a moto leather jacket, which by now you should already own or have at least eyed at your local vintage dig. You don't need to own more than one pencil skirt, because it's how you pair it for the occasion that makes it appropriate and different.

You may find the simplest and most inconspicuous item is the one that usually gets the most attention. It tends to be the one that produces pure empowerment, and procures the compliment that makes you blush. And if you are anything like me, you immediately dismiss by confessing that it wasn't expensive at all or that you had it forgotten in a drawer. The first example that comes to mind is a 'neck army' I made one day that I had some time to spend through my custom jewelry collection. It was a combination of a couple of rhinestone chokers, clunky and inexpensive, a platinum chain with a pendant of my daughter's initial and a string of black maxi sea pearls that I had modified inserting a silver custom-made skull. Definitely out of the ordinary, but by mixing high and low pieces, I was happily rewarded with many compliments. That's what I mean when I say "be creative, look outside the box and believe in it". Do it without expecting praise, though, because the non-intention is what brings the highest recognition.

An Italian closet is curated. It doesn't manifest itself after you switch a button. It is made of thoughtful acquisitions; classic, irreplaceable pieces, inherited and transmitted via generations. Fun ethnic accessories from vacations or memorable trips, and that piece from your father's closet that you eyed for a while and he hadn't realized had disappeared until that day you wore it at dinner.

Most of the times, the disruptive element was inexpensive, or caught your eye at the neighborhood vintage market, that whether simple or a statement piece, was meant to be yours.

It's a service tool just like the wrench in your car; you own it and keep it in reserve mode in case you ever need it. It saves you time and money when you receive a last-minute invitation, and serves to dress up or down the anonymous black dress without having to delve into a fast-fashion frenzy.

I learned so much from my mother who, with three children stuffed in a small Fiat 500 and plenty of afternoon activities, would always come back home to cook dinner for guests while simultaneously helping us with homework. She never had the need to buy anything to wear for the occasion, still she always managed to look pulled-together as her dinner guests would walk through the door. She'd look stylish while walking in and out of the kitchen to check the bass in the oven, or fix the flowers on the table. My siblings and I would be eating in

"Simplicity is the ultimate form of sophistication."
– Leonardo da Vinci

the kitchen, and while she'd hurried in and out tending to the guests, I would notice her dress, which she had worn on many previous occasions, but never seemed the same. It always looked like something new, something with an extra punch, so to speak. Finally, I'd notice it was the red embroidered jacket she had brought back from a trip to Petra, or the same Bakelite necklace from my grandmother's armoire that I had played with on many occasions.

Instead, if you own it, it produces a domino effect that goes something like this: I bought a simple insignificant accessory that caught my attention. I really didn't know if I was going to wear it, but I couldn't leave it. Now I keep finding different occasions to wear it, so it has already yielded the best ROI that I could possibly expect. It gathers attention from admiring people, and women also compliment me (a double win). Hence, my sense of style becomes a language that is admired and recognized. It's a short story with a very happy ending - an empowered and satisfied woman standing tall as the scene ends and the curtains close.

Some ideas of how to disrupt an outfit: One thing at a time is enough. It doesn't necessarily have to be an accessory, but any element used as a form of adornment that speaks to you in that moment, and makes you look unique and appropriate.

- Eliminate something from your look, say for example the pants. This is not an instigation to pornography, but if your tunic or shirt-dress is long enough to hide all it needs to cover while still leaving ample room as to not resemble that one-size-too-small bandage dress, or look like you've stretched your t-shirt into a dress, then just go for it. If done right, this can look feminine, sensual, but not intrusive. This doesn't apply for a Board review meeting or a school PTA gathering, though.
- Disheveled perfection would equal a lace skirt and an alpaca cardigan with elbow patches.
- The multiple uses of the scarf or 'scarf couture', like Barbara Hulanicki calls it in her latest production www.iconoclast.com. One of my mother's most cherished designer pieces was a silk Gucci scarf featuring a forest mushroom designed by the artist Accornero, which she used for years to the point of no return. No restauration efforts could save this scarf from its imminent death, except for framing it to be hung in the studio in memory of all the great moments it symbolized. And this scarf had many purposes. The creativity of utilizing this square piece of silk fabric went beyond the neck, where it usually lands; it got wrapped as a triangle over a blazer or as a long rectangle inside a blouse collar. My mom would wrap

it around the handle of her camel cross-body or use it as a belt through the loops of her favorite corduroy flares. I, too, infiltrated my mom's relationship with this special-edition Gucci scarf and inaugurated it at an unforgettable garden party by wearing it as a top, bowed in the front. From here on, it's a free falling adventure. Other uses for it might include bandanna and pareo, just think outside the box. Take notes from the Wabi-sabi model of finding beauty in things imperfect, modest and unconventional, and for example, add a knotted red bandana to a power suit.

- Wear paillettes (how we call sequins) for lunch, or if you're more daring, wear eveningwear during the day.
- Sleepwear during the day is as chic and dandy as it gets, which includes initialed pajamas and hand-embroidered silk slip-dresses, undergarments or night-gowns. It's all in the attitude. Wear it with the conviction that it's indeed a dress and nobody will ever know it was meant to be kept in the bedroom.
- Layering pants with dresses: if you're imagining the '70s that means Italian style was also 'a thing' in that decade. It's all in the contrast of the volumes - skinny pants, a wrap skirt, a shirt and a blazer.
- Embellished normcore: makes everything personal and adds character to the expected, the punchy punch. The first brand that started to break the rules was Prada. Mrs. Miuccia Prada is the queen of breaking the rules. Consuelo Castiglioni of Marni is pretty much running for office as the vice president of breaking the rules, and these were the only two of the major Italian brands until Alessandro Michele took the reign at Gucci and broke all the rules by bringing maximalism back to the stage. Besides the big names that we see in advertising, magazines, interviews, and pretty much everywhere, I discovered Furry LAB - an independent brand of slides lined with only recycled fur. "Not for all" says the tagline, the very first brand to line sporty slides like Birkenstock and Adidas. Orietta Marangoni is the creative director, creator and owner of Fur LAB; a shy designer, a pleasure to talk to and work with and, as expected, a genius.

How did Furry LAB begin?
OM – "By fluke…in 2013; by working for approximately twenty years in the fur-dressing sector, the accumulation and great quantity of worn fur is an inevitable consequence. How could all the

clothing articles, scarves, collars and borders be re-utilized? I began by covering one of my old pairs of Birkenstock, then my friends' shoes and so on…"

Do Furry LAB shoes break the rules?
OM – "Yes, the BRKfurry definitely break the rules and are contagious; a phenomenon that I cannot even explain today."

Can you still be sensual and feminine without wearing heels?
OM – "Well, I wouldn't say they are sensual, they are: different, comfortable and funny… Appreciated by women, and a bit less by men."

Trends and good taste: clash or follow the same path?
OM – "Definitely in contrast, trends go rarely hand-in-hand with fine taste. However, as we all know, fine taste is subjective."

The disruptive element makes you drift away from preppy and matchy-matchy, and keep it cool. Is the Furry Lab client rebellious or conservative? Or both?
OM – "BRKfurry customer is the mom that takes her children to school, the trend-setter fashionista and Milanese fine ladies. Recently, I was requested to make BRKfurry for all the women of a famous luxury brand, from the President's wife, to the style, marketing and sales office."

"Elegance is not catching somebody's eyes,
it's staying in somebody's memory."
– Giorgio Armani

95

What's an absolute NO in the Italian way of dressing?
OM – "Now everything is globalized, what is ugly is revalued as beautiful or cool… Definitely NO to wearing: junk, trademarks and/or initials of more or less famous brands."

- Headgear, like a turban, can be as sassy as a flapper girl inside a speakeasy. On Instagram, I discovered a brand called *Le Conturbanti*, designed and created by Stefania and Marta. The noun 'conturbanti' in Italian plays with a double entendre; the literal meaning being 'the girls with the turbans', and a provocative meaning being 'perturbing or unsettling'. As all the good things that have happened to me on Instagram, I interviewed the two girls behind the line because they gave me the bug of the turban, and I'd never worn one before."

How did Le Conturbanti begin?
LC – "*Le Conturbanti* was created by the meeting of two different, however complementary, individuals like the fantasies that characterize our headbands/turbans. We are both personal shoppers, and as you can imagine, always looking for inspirations and new trends. Nonetheless, the idea was stirred by a practical need. Since we are also moms of two lively "baby lions", we fight every day with the few minutes that we can take for ourselves, and the endless time we spend looking after our little devils. One day, after another bad hair day, we looked at each other and decided it was time to take measures. It was difficult to find on the market something that could perfectly reflect our personality, therefore we decided to conceive prototypes of turbans and let our fantasies loose. Since then, we have made various models for many friends, moms, etc., always in limited edition and at amateur level."

The turban brings one back in time to the age of the flappers in the Great Gatsby, and the Hollywood glamour of Greta Garbo; Do you need character to wear it?
LC, Stefania: "Of course! But many do not know that every woman has her own character."
LC, Marta for example, is also the voice of Dress in Blues and when she sings, she impersonates the stars of black music - Billie Holiday, Erykah Badu and Nina Simone.
LC, Marta: "Stefania instead is more at ease with the glamour of the '20s, and when she chooses the turbans' patterns, she always looks for soft and dreamy shades. We are two modern heroines, just like you!"

The turban also has a magic allure, like One thousand and One Nights; can it be worn like the queen wears the crown?

LC – "The turban is a crown! Whether made of precious fabrics or simple cotton, decorated with special stones or embroidered, it embodies the regalness of a queen."

Sometimes a hat is used to hide a bad hair day, but you don't hide with the turban, you actually make a statement. What are the characteristics of the perfect turban?

LC – "Yes, it's true! This is the reason why Le Conturbanti was born. Why hide due to a bad hair day? The characteristics of the perfect turban are essentially two: it must be practical and it must represent our personality through a color or pattern. It has an edge that goes beyond the fatuity of trends. How do we wear it as a disruptive element?"

LC, Stefania: "With a man's-cut suit and a baggy t-shirt. I love boyish style!"

LC, Marta: "Instead, I love wearing the turban with outfits in '90s style: "mom" jeans, striped t-shirt and an oversized bomber jacket!"

What's an absolute NO in the Italian way of dressing?

LC – "Here there are no banned styles, you just need to be aware of your body and age, without taking up identities that do not reflect you. You simply need to find the right colors and shapes that suit you and represent the setting for each phase of your life."

Talking about boyish, I wanted to touch upon the theme of the gamine look; Where ingénue meets tailored clothing, subtle natural makeup and rosy cheeks, short locks to frame the face and understated jewelry, in other words, Audrey Hepburn or Emma Watson. She is elegant and a bit naughty, feminine and attractive, she can be mischievous at times, but she is sensible. Her romanticism is veiled under some charm and shyness. It's a subtle style, understated and simple, where the disruptive element of a turban or a fierce stiletto, make a 'watch it, I am not predictable' kind of statement. Be warned, they always smile.

TEN

THERE IS NO SUCH THING AS PRETTY

"You don't have to be pretty. You don't owe prettiness to anyone. [...] Prettiness is not a rent you pay for occupying a space called 'female'."

This was audacious fashion editor Diana Vreeland's risqué appeal. She knew a thing or two about being born with attributes that didn't comply with the canons of 'pretty' and growing up with the burden of being the black swan of the family, when compared to her impeccably beautiful sister. Had she listened to the impartial judgement submissively, we wouldn't have a Harper's Bazaar or an American Vogue - the stature they are now. Her statement is as big as the indent she made in the way fashion is portrayed in print media. Her career in fashion began in the late '30s and flourished during the Mad Men era when women were pretty housewives wearing pink full skirts (you know how to read through my lines). A woman entrepreneur, a fashion editor not pretty in a conventional way, yet confident enough not to edit her thoughts, wasn't the norm in the world of publishing or in society. "The eye has to travel," was what High Priestess of Fashion Mrs. Diana Vreeland used to say, and it became a book and a documentary dedicated to her legacy. Because instead of looking for someone to idolize, she decided "I shall be that girl".

Those of you not familiar with Diana Vreeland, you may have stumbled upon the documentary *The Eye Has to Travel* or even the movie *Funny Face* – the latter being a spoof comedy mocking her life and her matter-of-fact visionary attitude. Mrs. Vreeland remains in history for her incomparable style, exquisite taste and legendary vision that helped Jackie Kennedy with her inaugural gown, and Diane Von Furstenberg's career. DV was a woman of character who owned her style and used instinct, experience and taste to make a mark, which included a profile not canonically pretty. By not following the rules, not listening to judgmental nonsense, Vreeland succeeded by facing social and prejudicial odds. Style with substance made her prevail in life.

I could take the radical route and mention the controversial vibes of the Pretty Hurts struggle in Beyoncé's song, or the humanitarian path of the HeForShe campaign supported by the U.N. and carried worldwide by young activist/actress Emma Watson. However, I want to keep it at the common understanding that a woman should be considered and embraced in the wholesomeness of her being, whether her nose line is crooked or she is not 20 anymore. Owning individual style is accepting one's own characteristics, body features and natural endowments with grace and confidence. Personal grooming, good manners and sense of humor are accessories that leverage the process of appreciation of those traits.

What fits you best and enhances your attributes, makes the best of your being, including the not-so-ideal nose lines, or the imperfectly aligned teeth, or that thigh gap unworthy of Instagram. Nose, teeth and thighs, as a matter of fact, have always been traits of my body that caused me pain as a teenager with all the insecurities that particular age brings. Had I only known I would come to regret it decades after, I wouldn't have let that affect me. Squeezing under the pressure of society's "beautiful girl" definition has only helped with noticing those same elements in someone else; pointing out negativity instead of reinforcing confidence.

Working on your personal style gives you the confidence of feeling at ease in your own skin, without falling in the trap of conformity. Finding someone else's #OOTD (Outfit of the Day) inspiring, creates a false sense of security. You feel forced to make a choice between trusting yourself, and trusting someone else who suggests you to wear those pieces that she looks best in via a series of altered social media pictures, with included link to a suggested purchase. An admirable and remunerated effort (creating the outfit, doing the photoshoot, blogging it, sharing it on social media) blatantly copied, can produce a disappointing final result on several levels. You may not like the fabrics, the cut could be ill-fitting, it may be overpriced for your acquisition power, and the look may be composed of items sold at fast-fashion chains. I am not dissecting or throwing shade on the blogging business because it would be anachronistic and unfair, what I'm pointing out is that the confidence of owning one's style goes beyond some conventional norms of "pretty", "amazing" and "sexy". There's no sexiness sought after in the Italian way - "mind-blowing," as Miranda Priestly of *The Devil Wears Prada* movie would say.

Dare for the unexpected, avoid blatant put-togetherness. Nothing is more boring for an Italian girl than the 'white picket fence' type housewife, the one that steps into high-voltage drama gear when invited to an event that calls for a dress code. The best answer to the monotony of the matchy-matchy is to go with your instincts. By now you have a good idea that you can respond to a dress code with your own drill, the same way that there are many ways of baking a brownie; Everyone's grandma's recipe is always better.

If cocktail attire means sheath dress and matching nude pumps to be accepted as pretty, it doesn't mean it's the standard. What if what's pretty for you looks tasteless for me? Think outside the box and dig into your closet, which by now has gotten the Italian treatment, and steer away from cookie-cutter looks. Right off the bat, you can choose to give the androgynous look to a tea-length skirt with a tuxedo jacket and a killer pair of lace-up heeled booties, or pair of brogues with a long silk spaghetti-strap dress and a turban. There's nothing more feminine, sensual, elegant, yet unconventionally pretty, than alluding to a woman's body instead of flaunting it shamelessly. By now, you know that an Italian man prefers to keep distance from the complications of a long beautifying process, he is naturally not attracted to a woman who doesn't "wake up like this".

The appreciation of a woman's beauty goes beyond socially imposed standards of 'pretty', the same way that Italian style goes beyond the country's borders. The exhausting race to whiter teeth, plumper breasts or wrinkle-free skin is not sensual, feminine or cool, which is what Italian swagger is known for. The easiness of accepting one's own imperfections, enjoying a succulent plate of spaghetti with a glass of wine, sunbathing like a lizard on the shores, are some of the little things that make 'la dolce vita'. If that interferes with the ultimate goal

"Style is knowing who you are, what you want to say, and not giving a damn."
– Orson Welles

101

of perfect abs or the absence of wrinkles around the eyes, there's always tomorrow for the sake of living in style with beauty, culture, history, family and sunshine.

Never feeling overdressed or overeducated, like dandy Mr. Wilde used to consider appropriate for a lady, is a very Italian thing to do. Remember to keep your chin high and walk gracefully as if you had a book on your head. With the last-minute invitation to a Sunday brunch on the terrace, or the annual office Christmas party, it shouldn't be a question of prettiness, but appropriateness. No need to waste your lunch break on a trip to the mall to get something, anything, in a frazzled state of panic and despair, seeing as how those pieces will most likely end up being returned the following day anyway. With a wardrobe built on essentials for your current lifestyle, all you need to do is first shop in your closet, then accessorize with confidence and personal touches. The process will land you compliments and produce an unbeatable boost of self-esteem.

The Italian girl is by nature imperfect and curious; she explores high-fashion windows and street markets alike. When you know your style and dress to please yourself first, you work around the odds to effortless-looking results. A deal, a vintage garment, a consignment rack, is a tickle, especially when you are not looking for something in particular. Your sense of style will give you the confidence of knowing, even without trying it on first, whether that dress fits you or not. You'll also not need a salesperson or a reality-show celebrity endorsing or validating it for you. The last thing you want to hear is: "you look so cute" (not unless you are 15).

Not paying attention to prettiness will empower you to approach the dress-for-your-age eyebrow-raising statement. To be told what we should or shouldn't wear, seems such an antiquated concept in a world in which everything is available at the snap of a finger. We can decide to look 17 again and defraud Mother Nature, trick the law of gravity with injections, relapse into mindlessly copying an image, a look, a persona that belongs to someone else. With a hand to our heart, all of the above will only render us weaker, and be unhelpful in the process. To empower ourselves and embrace who we are, we must be aware of the ineluctable change of our age like the seasons, and start dealing with what's appropriate for us and what is not.

The 'anything goes' or 'age is nothing but a number', doesn't really work universally. As aggressive and unapologetic as this may seem, the Italian way has some unspoken rules: mini-skirts shouldn't linger in any woman's wardrobe after the age of 50, which used to be 30 not a long time ago. Things have changed, we look younger than what our parents used to look like at our age, or to say it like Gloria Steinem: "This is what 40 looks like – we've been lying for so long, who would know?" However, there exists such a thing like common sense, the same way there is etiquette for how to properly sit at the table or host a dinner party.

Follow me on this shortcut: the fact that we mustn't abandon vertiginous heels for unforgiving comfortable ones or for a longer skirt hem, flirts with the pressure of looking pretty, and insinuates through the cracks of our minds. No matter your personal choices or taste, "[…] what is important in a dress is the woman who wears it," said Yves Saint Laurent.

And because I get overly passionate with these topics, I had a profound conversation about beauty and insecurity with Barbara Hulanicki, which was such a mind opener that I felt compelled to share. Hulanicki made an entrance into the world of fashion in 1964 with BIBA, it was revolutionary; the first lifestyle department store inspired by high-street life in swinging London. Her career has evolved through the years and taken her from fashion design to interior design, from drawing to photography, culminating with her 2012 OBE in recognition of her contribution to the world of esthetics.

We met, one hot summer afternoon, in her studio right in the heart of Miami Beach. I was in front of one of my icons. I had studied the unique case of the success of her business, born as an online catalogue with the collaboration of

"Being just "pretty" is an awful trap."
– Jane Birkin

her husband. I had first met her in Miami years ago, as creative director for a project of a Caribbean resort with Sol Kesner, and now I was in her studio filled with mannequins, books, many books, sketches, vintage findings, her most talented collaborator and her contagious genuine laugh.

I asked about what drives her:
BH - "I have to move forward. I love to learn what makes men with a vision, tick. They have this direct way of going from A to Z without any distractions along the way. Women are forever life-shopping. I find it fascinating to work through other people's minds, as I find I am so predictable to myself and I do find that boring."

We talked about the phenomenon of reality TV, celebrities and the pressure and urge to look photo-shopped, strobed, contoured at all times. I asked about how she had lived her fame in a time when she was not only revolutionary, but there were no street-style paparazzi, or 'it-girl' influencers.
"I never wanted the business to have my name so I would not have to be upfront. It is a full-time job being a celebrity. I like to be behind the spotlight, so I can on with the people watching. This is how you learn in my opinion, and you have to plod on, and I am a plodder.

On self-expression:
BH - "I get nostalgic about BIBA as it was so friendly and genuine, today everything has become so corporate. It is almost a sin to have an individual idea. That is why I love illustrations, as no one can interfere with his or her ideas when you are working."

The legacy of BIBA (Note to self: "Choose a job you love, and you'll never have to work a day in your life." – Confucius)
The strength of BIBA was that it was for wardrobe and lifestyle for the daily working girls. BIBA was not designed for fashion shows, or untouchable girls wearing untouchable clothes with exotic backdrops. In BIBA, the backdrop was the shop itself.

BIBA was created for the working girl, not for a fashion show. The store was an incredibly glamorous meeting point, and an esthetic experience. That was before street style took over fashion. Does beauty lie in imperfection or is it a continuous search for the perfectly polished image?

BH – "Street fashion. The décor in the shop was a backdrop to street type clothes. It had a friendly drawing room, comfortable for keeping the boys (partners) from leaving the shop. The customers were real girls who worked as typists and secretaries. Everybody had a job, there were very few students."

In this chapter of the book, I touch upon the delicate topic of how a woman can overcome the continuous demand for prettiness. How much do you see it attainable in this era of the selfie where no toe goes unfiltered?
BH – "Young girls have a lot of energy for improving their looks, other girls are influencing them and they are copying each other. It is later on when it becomes hard work."

Your drawings and portraits depict what lies behind a woman's veil of appearance, whether they are skinny or voluptuous, young or mature, the subjects look confident while embracing their assets. Do you believe every woman has a secret stash from where to get the courage to reach that level of freedom?
BH – "The BIBA drawings and BIBA photos were a guide to set your looks. In the '60s, there were no selfies and it was very bad form to be seen photographing each other, as the Japanese tourist were known to do."

You have collaborated with the late Elio Fiorucci. You contributed to his success in breaking the barrier of the conventional with transgression and anti-conformism. Can you see how trends must not be followed, but anticipated?
BH – "The collaboration was mutual. Fiorucci did it with an Italian flair and we did it with typically English background. It was all about revolting against the older generation and their antiquated values."

"Zest is the secret of all beauty. There is no beauty that is attractive without zest."
- Christian Dior

"You aren't pretty and you will never be pretty, but it doesn't matter because you have style,"
businesswoman turned icon of style, Iris Apfel, was told in her hey days by no less than Mrs. Loehmann
- founder of the eponymous department store.

P.S. THE JUICY LEFT-OVERS:
SOME THINGS YOU NEVER DO

Style has no rules.

We may not follow the rules. When it comes to style there is no right or wrong, but there are things you never do, like refuse a plate of pasta. I have used the analogy with food all along because food in Italy is not solely what keeps the family together, but an essential part of people's lifestyle. A household is not an Italian home without a bottle of olive oil, a flask of house wine, a box of coffee and a loaf of bread. The same amount of dedication, passion and research goes into a well-stocked kitchen, as it does into a carefully-curated armoire. The movement called, *Slow Living*, was born in the '90s to revitalize the way past generations had conducted their life by going back to follow natural rhythms in balance with nature. An Italian lifestyle is to be approached with a pace of easiness; it is not a life with no time for anything. There are no TV dinners, prepackaged meals, or fast fashion. Au contraire, living *la Dolce Vita* means living slowly, giving moments their purpose, whether it's choosing the applications for an evening gown or making risotto. It is appreciation; a sensorial occurrence to be fully experienced instead of being rushed through shortcuts because we are in a hurry.

WHAT'S YES

- Know the harmony of your body, your proportions, and don't forget to be you; not the wannabe version of you 20 years younger. Dressing with Italian style comes with rules, even though the final result seems as spontaneous as a bunch of small daisies blooming in the spring. It's a question of aesthetics, like making lasagna. It appears to be an easy 1-2-3 operation, but when you start following instructions, you realize that there's a reason why they appear so imperfectly and uniquely delicious. It is a process that needs timing, like the making of *la pomarola* (tomato sauce) a day ahead, grating *il parmigiano* (parmesan cheese, preferably aged for 24 months) on the spot, and the strict rule of 'no way you'll make them dive in a sea of melting mozzarella-like cheese'.

- Respect your style, be yourself, use your imagination and don't try hard while doing it. "Nothing makes a woman look as old as trying desperately hard to look young." – Coco Chanel

WHAT'S NO

- Flip flops are for taking a shower after swimming in the pool to avoid contact with lurking bacteria. It's a belief, and we take it as seriously as pasta's cooking time - not one extra minute, because we don't eat overcooked pasta.

When talking about flip flips, you'll have to read what Sally Perrin has to say about 'beachwear etiquette'. Sally Perrin, American-French style maven and creative mind behind the eponymous Perrin Paris luxury collection of leather goods, lives between Paris and LA to be with her family and run the business. She has shared her vision of a chic Italian woman through a recollection of vignettes of her vacation at Hotel Il Pellicano, in the Tuscany coast.

The summer holiday wardrobe etiquette according to Sally Perrin.
SP: "When I pack a bag to spend a weekend at my favorite Italian hotel, Il Pellicano, I select the most basic elements that are age appropriate and elegant. I do not own a pair of plastic flip flops; instead I will opt for Liwan sandals in dark green and gold from one of my favorite Left Bank shops in Paris for summer accessories. Baring too much skin is not appropriate, therefore, I will choose a high-waisted two-piece and a one-piece halter bathing suit to add to my Rimowa carry-on. I refuse to wear ripped jeans. These are completely out of fashion and in bad taste. I do not bring bling when traveling, I wear a good watch and add bangles and beads. I like sunning and swimming with a visor, but I will not wear a baseball cap. My Hermes visor is linen with leather trim, it has a fun tie knot on the back as added detail. To dress like a local, shop like a local. My selection will include items that are appropriate for the setting of choice. I will not wear my Mexican wedding dress that is appropriate in Careyes, while in Italy! I will not bring a plastic beach bag; instead a woven raffia and leather tote with wood trim from Perrin Paris. Finally, one thing I never do is bring a bad attitude. There is nothing worse than seeing guests in a beautiful setting act out with bad behavior!

Voilà."

- Cheap shoes are like bad dental hygiene, nothing good comes out of it. They ruin a good outfit and they kill a bad one, all after having procured blisters and joint pain. Normally we don't do cheap by principle, we don't even have a word for it in the dictionary. There are thrifty things that you can get away with, but it's not shoes. Especially, if you are thinking of buying cheap knock-offs, which is a recipe for disaster.
- Leggings as pants. We fell in love with them in *Flashdance* - that was the time in my life I was obsessed with leggings and leg warmers, but there's a role for everything. We can use our imagination, stretch gender boundaries, yet leggings outside of the dance studio and the '80s, should only be an accessory to frame an outfit, help you with a carnival costume or keep your legs warm in the winter. That's it. Then you have pantyhose, sensual and feminine like a pair of fishnet. Lastly, you have pants, which you actually wear as a garment.

And while on this topic, gym clothes - leggings, sweats, sneakers - are not to be worn outside of the gym environment, which we don't frequent that often anyway. *Athleisure* became a thing after Alexander Wang decided to sell athletic pants as a signature look, and was born with the intention of making luxury designer wear accessible. In decades past, something similar was attempted with sunglasses, small leather goods, makeup and perfumes, later followed by underwear lines, all resulting in a massive movement of aspirational aficionados.

- Don't wear a scrunchie hair tie outside of the bathroom, unless you are hipster teenager who loves indie rock bands and lives in Brooklyn or Portland.

I remember my grandmother never letting me go out without brushing my hair, and at least once a year we'd go to the beauty store, the *profumeria*, to buy expensive tortoise-shell hair accessories that I'd wear all year long for both, special celebrations and school. I have a vivid memory of the headbands, the clips and combs similar to the ivory ones used by the Flamenco dancers, although less embellished, which I would use to keep my hair away from my face in parted sides. There was never one time that the two sides would be symmetrical. Scrunchies and shower caps were relegated to the bathroom. You would have to leave them in there, even walking to the bedroom with them on was in bad taste, like coming down for dinner without a new clean shirt. On this, we must accept that young Prince George broke the rule by rocking his personalized robe to meet President Obama in the drawing room, but that's the future King of England we're talking about.

- Velour tracksuits and UGG boots is so 1999 Juicy Couture, that even Pam and Gela - the two founders - have moved on. It's an old genre and it smells of suburbia; it has now been defined under Athleisure, but that's a different story. We don't embrace trends as many fashion magazines would like us to.
- Avoid all-over logos, there's only one Moschino, and that includes Jeremy Scott's interpretation of him. Exuberance, maximalism, mixing patterns and color-blocking belong to a savvy Italian repertoire, but flashing bold logos are bad taste all around, whether it's design, décor or clothing. That has nothing to do with attending or watching the live stream of runway shows, which we will keep doing till death do us part. The result, though, will not be a preorder of a complete look from the brand, unless you are Anna Dello Russo and go behind the curtains, only to then leave the venue wearing the most applauded look from the runway show.
- Plastic see-through bra straps look as fake as when you are a tourist in Paris and take a picture with the Tour Eiffel, you just don't do that. A bra is supposed to make you feel naked, you shouldn't feel it and you shouldn't see it. However, it has an important function in making all your features look good and well placed.

There are times when it's OK not to wear a bra, and it's another of the few things we have in common with French girls. It's not uncommon to suntan topless while vacationing in the islands, with no other intention than avoiding tan lines. Likewise, because we are reticent with enhancing natural assets with plastic surgery, when sizes are moderate and everything can be kept under control, we don't mind wearing a T-shirt or a slip dress with no bra. Remember to smile always.

- Buy parures of costume jewelry and wear them together as a set. By now, you know that there is nothing set in stone with an outfit made the Italian way. Choose your accessories with rationale; Mix and match don't matchy-match. Costume jewelry should not be used the same, and unless you are a Diana Vreeland or Iris Apfel, split them up. The last thing you want is to look tacky or like we say in Italian, look like the Virgin of Montenegro covered in a slew of golden chains, bracelets and earrings where you could hardly see her clothing. You'll get better ROI by splitting them up; a competitive revenue in which the value of what you bought proportionally increases with how many times you wear it. Quality always wins over quantity. You are not a Christmas tree, so you need to last past December. You want to be a concert where the crowd requests an encore. One tip: the trick to make costume jewelry look burlesque is to mix them with fine jewelry. Make the top of shining metal, and the bottom of suede or silk, stones and shells.

- Know your size: there's nothing more vulgar than buying a size smaller than yours. Clothes should follow the natural movement of a woman's body, not constrict it. A *Basic Instinct* moment better be left in the boudoir. No matter the shape of your body, fashion offers something flattering for everyone; a savant choice is what makes the difference.

- Never try too hard: you don't want to look constructed. With your closet already strategized by now, you should be able to walk in and choose an outfit by the mood of the day, and come out comfortable in whatever you put on, disregarding what others will think. This is the best way to receive compliments. And when you do, you are genuinely surprised, because in reality it only took you 10 minutes to put the outfit together, and that's where the effortlessness comes from.

- You don't need to prove your status to anyone. Style is in your DNA and must be cultivated, nurtured and grown like a child. Taste comes from a combination of habits and rituals that go back to the time where dinners were not microwaveable, where you would listen to classical music and opera (since the majority of them are sung in Italian anyways), where you would listen to the classics being read on the radio after dinner, and where the bed sheets were dressed by crisp, ironed hand-embroidered linen.

- You don't need to mindlessly splurge to show your neighbor 'you've made it'. The secret is to still own the best cashmere sweater in town, pair it down with some basic cotton twill bermuda shorts, and if it's been used to shreds, add elbow patches, because some Wabi-sabi and appreciation of the ugly, never hurts. The same way you would hang your rare collection of studies by the Alinari brothers in the living room right next to your children's drawings. Low key, understated, no pretending or showing signs of acquired comfort or, as the French say, *nouveau riche* behavior.

-

"I was starving to see elegant women, that don't need much,
smart and sophisticated women are very simple dressers at the end"
- Alber Elbaz, on the inspiration of Lanvin's Spring 2015 collection

- Don't copy; get inspired by a life of style. Don't live in a street-style regulated life where the one who wears the 'it' bag, shoe, or has thousands of followers, rules. Life should go on unfiltered, it doesn't need five filters or a Vscocam edit to show put-togetherness or constructed taste. Think Miss Piggy: style is personality. The Italian girl is not going to be busted wearing yesterday's #OOTD worn by the influencer of the moment. Why? Because the Italian girl is not pretentious, au contraire, she is resourceful and knowledgeable, and can differentiate Alpaca from cashmere, even while blindfolded, just by the touch and good sartorial cut behind the seams. All you need is to be curious, do research, watch (or attend if you can) a few runway shows of the designers that most inspire you, not the ones that bloggers and influencers are mad crazy about, don't be influenced by other people's biased opinions. Then read, keep yourself up to speed, go to your favorite boutique before actually having to make a purchase, make sure you are on the same page with the buyer or owner's style, and then get the pieces you want before anyone else.

- Don't use the way you dress to hide behind the mask of another social group. Think *Gossip Girl* for example, you are either Blair Waldorf or you are not. The best little sis Jenny could ever do, was try to climb the ladder and pretend, from Gumbo to Park Avenue, a one way trip with a harsh return. Your style is who you are and wherever you are now. Own it. Embrace the assets you do have instead of whining for the ones you lack. Be happy and proud of what you have and can do, and if you can't vacation in Formentera with Lapo Elkan and crew, you will not serve jail time or go to hell. Gentility is the idea, don't try to be of aristocratic descent because you went to the same private school as some aristocrats, or pretend to be Italian if your uncle's great-grandfather came from Italy at the beginning of last century. Those things are not cool, and you, as an Italian girl, are cool.

- Never buy in bulk. Rome wasn't made overnight and the Roman Empire was one of the strongest and most extensive of all times. Have you ever found yourself in a mood where you think: I want to start dressing like Margherita Missoni, organize a closet party, get rid of everything and start a new life full of knitwear? Normally, those spur-of-the-moment thoughts are the perfect recipe for disaster and disappointment. I have done it myself one too many times with my wardrobe, with terrible results. But nothing that couldn't be fixed after a few years and a good chunk of money spent. Although, when I was 16 I did something silly that still to this day has an impact on my life. My mother once received a thank you note from an English Lady, I was so impressed by her cultivated handwriting that I decided I would change mine, point blank. I remember long evenings trying to learn to do a perfect F and B, starting with my signature and moving on to rewriting entire passages from the newspaper. The result is that now I am the only one who understands my cursive, and sometimes, on special sunny days, my mother does too; perhaps out of her good maternal instincts.

- Don't do department stores, unless it's the private club or the personal shopping experience. The concept of the department store is as alien to an Italian girl as it is for an American to understand that Italians don't drink cappuccino after meals. There is only one in Milan, called *La Rinascente*, and that's about it, which goes to show that it didn't grow roots in our culture. It is not another way to be posh and act eccentric; on the contrary, the truth is that it's intimidating. There are too many aspects of a department-store experience that are not pleasant. Racks are filled with too many sizes and choices that you can't appreciate the styles, the message or the inspiration. The sales persons are lurking around you, whether at Macy's or Bergdorf's, different manners, but they still satellite around you in a most uncomfortable way. It all goes back to that concept of slow living and the attitude we have towards buying something. When we decide to buy a dress, we have made a decision based almost on a couture-level experience; the fabric, the designer, the style, the colors, the originality, we have seen it going down the runway, seen close-ups, then we want the experience to go with it. We want to try it on, feel it and twirl in it with a certain dose of privacy, comfort and complicity, all of which we are accustomed to finding in a boutique. I must confess that in my 20 years in the States the only time I have purchased a wardrobe item from a department store, a pair of heels to be precise, was to meet Sarah Jessica Parker at the solo appearance she had in Aventura Mall while on tour to first introduce her shoe collection.
- Don't plunge into trends. We set them, not indulge in them.
- Don't do cheap. Cheap looks cheap no matter what.
- Serial cotton underwear: there's no excuse for wearing cotton granny panties with pugs and cherries on them. Those 'buy five for $20' deals from Target need to be avoided like the flu.

Underwear has constrictions that are to be taken almost religiously. The fact that it's not seen in public doesn't mean it can be mismatched or ill-fitting. My grandmother says: "make sure you have clean underwear, and comb your hair before being seen in public, because you never know." I was brought up in a world where it was OK for a girl to dream of her Prince arriving to meet her on a white horse, so you couldn't look disheveled. There's only one Cinderella, the rest of us must look decent at all times (because you never know).

- Tights with holes, unkept or mismatched socks of inferior quality. Tubular mid-calf white socks from the gas station should never be purchased. In fact, there's no reasonable use an adult should find for them, except for temporarily isolating the draft coming in from a malfunctioning window in your home.
- Never wear off-the-rack items without having them altered. Unless it's a red carpet mishap or an accident, there should never be any permanent safety pins, rolling up, or tape on sleeves or pants. A good seamstress, or tailor, is like that apple a day that keeps the doctor away.
- Don't share your seamstress' contact details, keep it under guard like your plastic surgeon's name.

Adopting an Italian style can be done with the right dose of playfulness. You have to maintain that appreciation for slow living. Enjoy the pleasures of the little things, practice, and mix high and low, couture with modest simplicity; it's intelligent luxury, the one that is first a state of mind. Don't go by the book; use imagination and a certain dose of aplomb in knowing that you can wear sequins in the daytime and never look too dressed up. Understand that you can dress the Italian way no matter where you live, how old you are or how much money you have.

AUTHOR BIOGRAPHY

Francesca Belluomini is a quick-witted and unapologetic fashion veteran and a style savant. She has lived in Miami long enough to know not to blink when peacocks cross the street, but is originally from Viareggio, Tuscany, the same region where local notables Marquis Emilio Pucci and Guccio Gucci were born.

With a degree in Fashion Sociology and a master's in Mass Media and Communication from the University of Florence, foundations which formed her notorious unpretentious taste, Francesca has dedicated her entire career to fashion. Her career and personal life choices have led her to live in fashion capitals like Milan, Paris and London, and sealed her unmistakable knack for mixing sartorial garments, local market finds and vintage.

People would always compliment her chic style and would want to dress like her. They would admire her ability to put things together with a nonchalant elegance. She worked to capture the essence of her process, extracted a concentrate, and created the tools for every woman to achieve this same flair by adapting their wardrobe to the Italian style. This is how her book 'The Cheat Sheet of Italian Style" came to life.

SocialMiami.com, CBS Local Miami, TrustedClothes.com and Italian e-zine www.DDmag.it are some of the latest publications that have enjoyed her sharp and witty fashion writings.

You can find her on www.FrancescaBelluomini.com where she voices her thoughts in a more intimate and personal manner.

ABOUT FRANCESCA

The power of image dominates everyday lives and personal style is its immediate language, no matter where you live, how old you are or how much you have. *The Cheat Sheet of Italian Style* bridges the disconnect between a cluttered closetful of meaningless clothing to a curated wardrobe, empowering the reader one strut at a time with humor, confidence and nonchalance.

Francesca Belluomini, born and raised in Italy, is a fashion veteran and style savant who for the past decade has called sun-drenched Miami Beach her home although Milan is still where her heart resides. From her grandmother's armoire to a major in Fashion Sociology; from seasons in showrooms in Milan to a master in Communication; from styling runways to branding and retail for international designers; these have all forged the solid foundation to her fashion expertise and signature style.

As a vivid writer and speaker, Francesca's anecdotes and life lessons enthrall the audience, and put a heartfelt spin to the world of fashion and glamour. She's passionate about shifting women's views that a life of style is frivolous and a deterrent to personal growth. Instead, she emphasizes on style and luxury being a state of mind at its core, and teaches the reader the step-by-step process how to find their inner effortless-chic style, the Italian way. Good news is: you don't need to be Italian.

Francesca's Memberships and Participations:

Fashion Group International
South Florida Bloggers
Women Speaker's Association
Femfessionals
Non Fiction Authors Association

Francesca's Writings and Contributing Columns:

SocialMiami.com
DDmag.it
TrustedClothes.com
Miami.CBSLocal.com

To learn more about and interact with Francesca Belluomini visit:

Website: www.francescabelluomini.com
LinkedIn: www.linkedin.com/in/francescabelluomini
Twitter: twitter.com/chicfbdotcom
Instagram: www.instagram.com/chicfbdotcom

CPSIA information can be obtained
at www.ICGtesting.com
Printed in the USA
BVHW01s1722300418
514822BV00026B/1295/P